Praise for the plays of Neil LaBute

This Is How It Goes

"[LaBute's] most sophisticatedly structured and emotionally complex story yet, this taut firecracker of a play about an interracial love triangle may do for liberal racism what David Mamet's *Oleanna* did for sexual harassment."

—JASON ZINOMAN, *Time Out New York*

"This prolific playwright . . . has topped even his own scary self in this unrelentingly perilous, disgracefully likeable 90-minute marvel about race, romance and our inability to know everything about just about anything . . . The only unambiguous thing about this astonishing play is its quality." —LINDA WINER, *Newsday*

"The most frank, fearless look into race relations from a white dramatist since Rebecca Gilman's *Spinning into Butter*."

—ELYSA GARDNER, *USA Today*

Fat Pig

"The most legitimately provocative and polarizing playwright at work today." —DAVID AMSDEN, *New York*

"The most emotionally engaging and unsettling of Mr. LaBute's plays since *Bash* . . . A serious step forward for a playwright who has always been most comfortable with judgmental distance."

"One of Neil LaBute's subtler efforts . . . Demonstrates a warmth and compassion for its characters missing in many of LaBute's previous works [and] balances black humor and social commentary in a . . . beautifully written, hilarious . . . dissection of how societal pressures affect relationships . . . Astute and up-to-the-minute relevant."

"Will make you squirm in your seat. It's theater without novocaine [from] an author with a uniquely truthful voice."

The Mercy Seat

"[A] powerful drama . . . LaBute shows a true master's hand in gliding us amid the shoals and reefs of a mined relationship."

"Though set in the cold, gray light of morning in a downtown loft with inescapable views of the vacuum left by the twin towers, *The Mercy Seat* really occurs in one of those feverish nights of the soul in which men and women lock in vicious sexual combat, as in Strindberg's *Dance of Death* and Edward Albee's *Who's Afraid of Virginia Woolf?*"

"An intelligent and thought-provoking drama that casts a less-than-glowing light on man's dark side in the face of disaster . . . The play's energy lies in LaBute's trademark scathing dialogue."

—ROBERT DOMINGUEZ, New York *Daily News*

The Shape of Things

"LaBute is the first dramatist since David Mamet and Sam Shepard—since Edward Albee, actually—to mix sympathy and savagery, pathos and power."

—DONALD LYONS, *New York Post*

"LaBute . . . continues to probe the fascinating dark side of individualism . . . [His] great gift is to live in and to chronicle that murky area of not-knowing, which mankind spends much of its waking life denying."

—JOHN LAHR, *The New Yorker*

"*Shape* . . . is LaBute's thesis on extreme feminine wiles, as well as a disquisition on how far an artist . . . can go in the name of art . . . Like a chiropractor of the soul, LaBute is looking for realignment, listening for a crack."

—JOHN ISTEL, *Elle*

Some Girl(s)

"No contemporary American playwright is more brilliant than LaBute at dramatizing mankind's passion for Ignorance. *Some Girl(s)* is yet another astute demonstration of his uncanny ability to draw pure water from the most poisoned of wells . . . Guy exhibits a deep-seated misogyny that he cannot see in himself but cannot help making visible to others. LaBute is the only one of his playwriting peers to fully understand and dramatize this psychological fillip, which is why his plays are so complex and unnerving."

—JOHN LAHR, The New Yorker

"[A] pungent little morality play."   —JORGE MORALES, Village Voice

"Some girls get revenge, and some guys deserve what they get. That's the message in Neil LaBute's entertaining, sleekly written new comedy . . . As messages go, this one has been around since *Medea*. But LaBute, who likes to chronicle the underside of urban couplings, gives this version his usual sardonic edge along with some newfound depth . . . Here, he works carefully and successfully to portray a range of sexy, smart women."

—ALEXIS GREENE, The Hollywood Reporter

Neil LaBute

WRECKS *and other plays*

NEIL LABUTE is a critically acclaimed playwright, filmmaker, and fiction writer. His controversial works include the plays *bash: latter-day plays*, *The Distance from Here*, *The Mercy Seat* (Faber, 2003), *Fat Pig* (Faber, 2004), *Autobahn* (Faber, 2005), *This Is How It Goes* (Faber, 2005), *Some Girl(s)* (Faber, 2006), and *In a Dark Dark House* (Faber, 2007); the films *In the Company of Men* (Faber, 1997), *Your Friends and Neighbors* (Faber, 1998), *Nurse Betty*, *Possession*, and *The Wicker Man*; the play and film adaptation of *The Shape of Things* (Faber, 2001); and the short-story collection *Seconds of Pleasure*.

Other works by Neil LaBute available from Faber and Faber

In the Company of Men

Your Friends and Neighbors

The Shape of Things

The Mercy Seat

Autobahn

Fat Pig

This Is How It Goes

Some Girl(s)

In a Dark Dark House

Wrecks

and other plays

Wrecks

and other plays

Neil LaBute

Faber and Faber, Inc.
An affiliate of Farrar, Straus and Giroux
NEW YORK

FABER AND FABER, INC.
An affiliate of Farrar, Straus and Giroux
19 Union Square West, New York 10003

Library of Congress Cataloging-in-Publication Data
LaBute, Neil.
    Wrecks and other plays / by Neil LaBute. — 1st ed.
        p.   cm.
    ISBN-13: 978-0-86547-970-8 (pbk. : alk. paper)
    ISBN-10: 0-86547-970-4 (pbk. : alk. paper)
    I. Title.

    PS3612.A28W74 2007
    812'.54—dc22

                                                    2006102858

Designed by Gretchen Achilles

www.fsgbooks.com

10   9   8   7   6   5   4   3   2   1

For Walter and Denise, who continue to
bravely swim upstream through my river of work

Never say you know the last word about any human heart.

HENRY JAMES

How many times can you get fucked in how many different ways?

KRISTIN HERSH

Contents

Preface: Stage Orphans

What you hold in your hands is a strange little collection—as I suppose all "collections" are by their very nature—a group of short plays and monologues that span a certain number of years in my career but are not distinctly linked by theme, concept, actors, or even venue. In fact, the thing that best distinguishes these eight playlets is that most of them (with the exception of *Wrecks* and *Falling in Like*) were written for someone or something—an actor or an event was the occasion for most of their births, which is rarely if ever the case in my other writings. As you can see from reading their varied production histories, many of the pieces included here have enjoyed just one night on the stage, at a benefit or a festival or the like. Plays are such fragile things—strong, also, to be sure—but they live in the here and now of their presentation before a live audience, and it always seemed unfair somehow for so many of these little creations to live their lives out only on my hard drive and in the memories of a small audience somewhere.

I feel very lucky to now be able to present this assortment to the reader—each one is too short to be published on its own, but to have found a kind of foster home for these stage orphans is a nice thing indeed.

Wrecks is a slightly different creature in that I wrote the play as a further investigation into the Greek theater and, more specifically, how the themes and plots of those amazing plays might be utilized in a contemporary way. This play follows closely a model that I established for myself with *bash*, and it was a pleasure to take many elements from the myth of Oedipus and apply them to my own little story of a man and the one great love of his life. That play found a first home in a rather unlikely place—at the Everyman Palace Theatre in Cork, Ireland, under the artistic directorship of Pat Talbot. Pat is a wonderful, towering man who bears a happy resemblance to Oscar Wilde; we became friends when I was in Dublin directing a production of *bash* at the Gate Theatre, where Pat was at the time technical director, and an offer of his to "work together" came to fruition in 2005 when Cork was chosen as the European Capital of Culture for that year. Pat reached out to me, saying this was the perfect chance to collaborate on a show—the one play I had on deck that I felt could successfully make the journey to another country was the solo show *Wrecks*. I was beyond lucky when it came to casting the piece—Ed Harris read it and was intrigued enough to say yes and make what turned out to be a two-year trek into this character's soul (a second staging of the play took place a year later at the Public Theater in New York, thanks to Oskar Eustis, the artistic director there). The greatest compliment I can give Ed is that it is now impossible for me to imagine another person in the role and, while it was not written for him, I have rarely seen such a gripping and successful melding of actor and material. Movie posters will occasionally proclaim that some actor *is* so-and-so, but that really is the case with Mr. Harris and the role of "Edward Carr." He is transformed on the stage, and if you're fortunate enough to see him do his work there—only three plays in the past twenty years, so don't hold your breath—you should count yourself blessed. He is someone who can be mentioned in the same sentence as Burbage or Kean or Booth or Brando or the like. I gush because he deserves it, not because I'm a gusher by nature.

Beyond *Wrecks*, there's a little something for everyone in this

Whitman's Sampler of a collection—a bittersweet tale from 9/11 (written with my dramatic doppelganger, Paul Rudd, in mind), a few nice monologues (given life by such terrific performers as Josh Hamilton, Mos Def, and Lauren Ambrose), and two pieces that work to dismantle that fascinating theatrical device known as "the fourth wall." There is even a new monologue that has yet to be performed publicly, but I wanted to include it here so that it really feels like you're getting a bargain deal; hey, kids, be the first in your school or neighborhood to perform the woman who waits for a man who may never come to meet her! *Falling in Like* is a lovely little study in self-delusion and should make many readers and most actresses very happy.

I trust you'll enjoy this group of bastards who have waited to find a home. I can't help but think of this motley crew with the same affection that I usually afford to something like Edward Gorey's *The Gashleycrumb Tinies*; they are like a gaggle of ghouls collected happily around my feet, and I adore them all the more because of their "outsider" status. I sincerely hope that you will as well.

Wrecks

For Charles Isherwood—who should've known better

Production History

Wrecks had its world premiere on November 23, 2005, at the Everyman Palace Theatre in Cork, Ireland. Artistic Director: Patrick Talbot. Director: Neil LaBute. Scenic and Costume Design: Klara Zieglerova. Lighting: Paul Denby. Sound: Mark Donovan. Production Manager: Mary Michele Miner.

EDWARD CARR Ed Harris

Wrecks had its U.S. premiere on October 10, 2006, at the Public Theater in New York City. Artistic Director: Oskar Eustis. Director: Neil LaBute. Scenic and Costume Design: Klara Zieglerova. Lighting: Christopher Akerlind. Sound: Robert Kaplowitz. Production Managers: Cole Bonenberger and Mary Michele Miner.

EDWARD CARR Ed Harris

Characters

EDWARD CARR, nearly sixty, a man of business

Setting

A funeral home somewhere outside Chicago

Silence. Darkness.

*Lights up to reveal a room shrouded in shadows. At the center—
a casket, covered in flowers. On a table nearby are several
photographs of a woman, framed.*

*At the back of the room, an archway opens out onto a different
area, well lit. The sound of people milling about.*

*A man nearby—*EDWARD CARR—*pulls a pack of Camels out of his
sensible black jacket. He lights one up as he waves away a puff
of smoke. Smiles as he looks about.*

EDWARD . . . hard to kick, you know? Habits, I mean. This stuff—
   and I don't care what it is you're into, candy, the drugs,
   whatever—once you give yourself over to something, it's,
   well . . . it's a devil of a deal to beat it. Believe you me.

*Another puff as he listens to the sound of the folks in the next
room.*

EDWARD I've been doing this, sucking these babies down for . . .
   since I was a kid and, trust me, that was not yesterday!
   I mean, I'm not *ancient*, it wasn't before television—or
   dinosaurs, as my grandson likes to say—but it's been a while.
   And I know, I *know*, I see the commercials and read the ads
   and all that, I do, but I've never been able to give 'em up for
   more than a day. Well, day and a half one time, but that was

Wrecks   5 it. I think I even snuck one then—during my *thirty-six* hours on the wagon! Or "cold turkey," actually, that's what they call it in smoker's language—I had myself a drag or two even when I was cold turkey. Just couldn't help it. When you're hooked, you're hooked, not much you can do about it. (*Grins.*) Hey, I'd quit if they'd stop making 'em taste so damn good! Seriously . . .

He looks for a place to flick his ashes—notices some potted plants nearby. Crosses and uses the dirt. He stops and looks around, listening for a moment. He takes a drag. Turns back toward that other room.

EDWARD God, listen to me in there! I sound like a complete ass, don't I? Yeah, it's okay, you don't have to say anything. I can hear myself going on like some sort of . . . (*Beat.*) Who ever uses the word "indeed" unless you're at a funeral or something? Poor guy comes over to say "She was a wonderful woman" and I go with, "Indeed, she was." *"Indeed"?!* Oh well, I'm sure I meant it when I said it . . . ahhh, what're you gonna do, huh? Standing in some funeral parlor with dozens of people around you, trying to cram all her *lifetime* into a few handshakes . . . You throw a couple words like "indeed" in there and hope for the best, that's what you do . . . can't be helped. (*Laughs to himself.*) Just trying to be honest here, get some of my feelings across, and there's not a thing wrong with that. Is there? To be open. Vulnerable. In touch with your emotions and, you know . . . all that other crap. I think it's a very good thing . . .

He points toward the picture of a woman on a table.

EDWARD *She* taught me how. Mary Josephine. She did, absolutely.
I don't know why I'm saying that, using her full name like I just
did—I mean, of course I'm gonna in my thing there, my,
whatchamacallit that I'm doing tomorrow? The eulogy. That's
obvious that I'd do it there, but not in life. Not during our time
together, uh-uh. No. She was always just "Mary Jo" to me . . .
or "Jo." Well, "Jo-Jo" sometimes, when I was being cute, or up
in the bedroom—you don't need to know too much more
about that, thank you very much! I think I come from a
different, you know, *generation* than most *people* do on that
particular subject, so, no. You can't open the paper today
without reading about how so-and-so is doing it with what's-
her-name, or how much they love doing such and such. *And*
made themselves a videotape, which is available off the
computer there, for just *$19.95*! Good God, what've we
become? Huh? Buncha savages, just sitting around the
campfire and trying to keep one another entertained! And for
what? I do not give a damn how you like doing it, I really don't,
or even if you do, *if* you like doing it at all. Who cares? Jesus,
that's your business, it absolutely is, so, please, keep it to
yourselves, you know? (*Smiles.*) At least not here, anyway.
During this. That's not very appropriate . . . (*Beat.*) My wife's
dead, have a bit of respect.

Hears the sound of the group again. Listens.

EDWARD I must be doing something right in there! Listen to 'em
all, crying and everything. Big laugh now and again. All shook
up. Well, that's good, they should be, she was a lovely
woman. Absolute heaven come to earth and squeezed into
human form—hey, I'm not gifted, don't have a touch of the

poet in me, first to admit that, but she was. An absolute
angel.

He looks inside the room, studying the others. Smiles.

EDWARD . . . yeah, they're all crying now, sure. Why not? They got
an audience. Makes sense, it's what most people do. Let it all
out in public and everybody gives you a hankie and their best
wishes. So be it. Not me, though, no thank you. Not that I
didn't cry, mind you, when she went. My Jo-Jo. Oh no, I
sounded like . . . *Heidi*, probably. You know, that little girl from
the fairy tale? Up in the Alps and whatnot, with the
grandfather and all . . . doesn't matter. I heard that story
when I was a kid and I recall her crying a great deal. Or maybe
that was the film . . . with Shirley Temple in it. Now, *that* kid
was crying all the time, any movie they put her in. They
exploited the shit outta her, forgive my language, but they did;
I read somewhere a piece on her, an obituary or something—
maybe not, she may not even be dead, I don't really know—
an article that described her childhood, all glamorous and
whatnot from the outside, to the casual observer, like you or I
might be—see, Hollywood has a way of doing that, from
everything I've heard—but she was quite the very abused
young woman. Not like Judy Garland or anything, not that bad,
with the pills and all, but still . . . like some orphan kid that
gets passed around from family to family, that's how those
studios treated her. Like that. And for a child, I mean, some
young kid, there isn't anything out there much worse than
that . . . being all alone and not loved. *Un*loved. Believe you
me. (*Beat.*) And, hey, I oughta know, right? I mean, that's me
all over. An orphan. Oh yeah, I grew up that way, in the foster

Neil LaBute

care system, I sure did. Just outside of Coeur d'Alene, Idaho, and never knew my *parents*. That's my life, in a nutshell . . . but, hey, this isn't about me. Not today. Well, it is, I mean, a *bit*, but we're supposed to be honoring the memory of my Mary Jo, so I'll shut up for a minute here, let you say your amens or whatever it is you do . . .

The man sits on a small bench, bowing his head for a moment. Snaps up when he hears more noise—shakes his head very disapprovingly as he begins to speak.

EDWARD   . . . see, I cried when I should've. *In* the moment. When it happened, rather than now when the world is staring at me and expecting it. I mean, that's hypocritical, I guess, 'cause listen to me there, I've got that sound going, I definitely do . . . a catch in my voice . . . listen . . . (*Waits.*) Hear it? Right there as I'm talking to her niece. Just . . . now. "The day we met . . ." (*Smiles.*) It's expected, what can I tell you? And I do feel it, I *absolutely* do, but it's still manufactured. You know? *After* the fact. Not like on the day, right as I lost her. There's nothing like that, not a thing in your life that's anything like that moment. I mean it. Nothing that you do while you're living can prepare you for a time like that one—when you stop. Being, I mean. Existing. Because, you know, you only do it once, and even if you're just seeing it, like, over somebody's shoulder . . . well, there ain't anything like it. (*Beat.*) And that wasn't me, some passerby. No, this was my wife, the lady in my life for over thirty years I'm talking about here. My right arm, my, umm . . . better half. Apple a my eye and, and any other . . . *cliché* you care to name. Jo-Jo. Oh yeah, I cried when it happened, believe you me . . . bawled like a goddamn *second*

grader and I'm not ashamed of it. I did indeed. (*Laughs.*)
Ahhh, there's that word again! "Indeed." Well, it just goes to
show you . . .

The man wipes at his eyes—a tear or two forming there.

EDWARD . . . what're you gonna do? I'm an emotional guy.
I mean, now. I am *now*, thanks to Mary Jo. But always in an
understated way, not blubbering in the grocery store so
everybody can pat me on the back and make me feel better,
no. I do it in my own time, within the privacy of my own home.
Or thoughts. Like this here . . . (*Beat.*) And that's fine with me.
Just so I do it, as long as I don't bottle it all up, like I used to,
that's what Jo-Jo taught me. Taught me how to get it out, in a,
ummmmm . . . an "appropriate" fashion. She loved that word,
"appropriate." Heard this Oprah Winfrey—you know, that black
lady on the TV—she said it one time and Jo ran with it like
she was a *fullback* heading for the end zone! Good God . . .
how she loved all that psychology stuff! Buying those self-help
books and listening in on the chat shows, all of that junk,
even the ones with men doing the talking. Not Phil Donahue
since he retired, but lots of those other fellas, you know,
ummmm . . . well, I don't know their names, but some of
those guys. The bald one and that other man. Mary Jo
absolutely adored those things. Oh yes, indeed she did . . .
(*Grins.*) Shit, there I go again, listen to me! I guess I use it
more than I thought I did. A word like that one . . . *indeed*
I do.

*The man smiles as he pulls another cigarette out of his jacket
pocket.*

Neil LaBute

EDWARD . . . you okay? I won't smoke if you're—I don't know what you're supposed to do in that situation, because who's gonna say something to a widower, right? Not anybody in their right mind. (*Lights it.*) I could probably go down to a car lot and drive outta there with a new model today, for free! (*Beat.*) Well, I'd have to go to the right one, of course, one familiar with my *situation*, but still . . . I bet I'd get a hell of a deal, a day like this. Not that that's what's in my head, mind you, as I'm standing in there—it's not, I promise it's not—I'm just pointing out a fact about people and how they react to grief. We tend to give folks shit, you know, offer 'em up presents and food and whatever . . . thinking it'll make 'em feel better. Or to make ourselves feel better, yeah, that's probably it. Instead of an honest look or spending that extra hour with 'em, we bring along a nice *casserole* and think that'll do the trick. God, we are a funny bunch, aren't we? Us folks. Yep . . . we sure are.

He stops and thinks for a long moment. Nodding. Pats his jacket pocket.

EDWARD . . . eulogy oughta go off without a hitch, thank Christ! I think I got everything in there. I'm gonna mention the—all her clubs and stuff—that Mary Jo was a part of, because people like hearing about that. What you did with yourself while you were here. Like, it's not enough to just get along with it and feed yourself and find somebody to love and have children and all that—no, apparently it's necessary to have *done* something with your life, too. What *they* consider is worthwhile. Seriously, I was talking to this woman earlier, don't remember her name, it's Cheryl something, she's the

one with the hat on and the red dress. Right there. *Red* . . .
go figure. (*Shouts.*) It's a *viewing*, sweetheart, not the Spring
Fling down at the American Legion! Even a dark *brown*
would've been appreciated!! (*Smiles.*) Ahhhh, whatever, she's
here, I guess, ol' Cheryl is, and so that's something. Anyhow,
she and I were talking out front before we got started and
she's pumping me for information, drilling me about all of Jo-
Jo's many accomplishments and this and that, and always
with the, "Yes, but what did she do with her life? What did she
do?" Like four kids, a husband, and about *seventeen*
branches of our business across five states isn't enough! No,
she keeps staring up at me with that two-dollar lipstick of hers
and saying, very loudly, "Yes, dear, but what did she *do*?"
Well, I'll tell you what she did, you wanna know so *damn* bad;
Jo-Jo spent more of her free time regretting her life—first half
of it, anyway, before she met me—wishing it'd turned out
differently, had all worked out some *other* way, that's what she
did . . . but it's nobody's goddamn business, and certainly not
ol' Cheryl's. (*Beat.*) So I penciled in a few of her memberships
and ribbons she won at different things, the Rotary Club and
crap, and that'll be that . . . that's why I'll drone on for so long
tomorrow. When I'm talking up there. Not that people care,
mind you, God no, Mary Jo was loved by this community! I
mean, if there's a word that suggests more than that, bigger
than "loved," well . . . that's what she was. "Beloved," I guess
that would be more like it. *Be*-loved, and even that might
come up a bit short. Mary Josephine Carr (maiden name
Delaney) was a, umm . . . ohh, what's that one term? It's . . .
(*Thinks.*) A pillar of society. I'm not kidding you. I mean, you
might not be able to tell by looking at her there . . . (*Indicates*

Neil LaBute

a photo.) . . . but Mary Jo was . . . well, she was *something.* Honestly. She was.

The man finishes up his cig and stubs it out. Stretches.

EDWARD . . . I'm sure you know—I mean, are probably whispering to yourselves—the age difference. Right? Believe me, I'm over it, so say what you're gonna. I've heard it all, trust me! *Yes,* she was a bit older than me—fifteen years, most months, although it was fourteen from January to March—but I never really felt it when we were together, I didn't. And especially not during the beginning, which is a whole . . . well, not that many people know how we got started, Jo-Jo and me. See, we became a regular town fixture, most of our lives, but back in the day we were *quite* the item. Of gossip, I'm saying. Oh, yes *indeed.* (*Smiles.*) Probably could've landed ourselves a spot on one of those talk shows, way back when! You see, whether any of you believe in it or not, and I'm not saying I do either, but . . . on that one occasion, in this *particular* instance, it was love at first sight, it really was. On my part, at least. Well, with a fair bit of lust in there, too! She was . . . my God, if you could've seen this woman, I mean, when she was forty? Forget about it. Knock the socks off any girl on any street corner—and I'm saying all up along Michigan Avenue—on any day of the year. *Any.* And this is a forty-year-old woman I'm speaking of here! Jo-Jo was a, well, simply put . . . she was a pearl that fell to this planet like some tear outta the eye of almighty Christ himself, up there on the cross—and I don't think it's sacrilegious in any way to say that, I really don't. I may not be so great with the words, I've already told you

Wrecks

that—I mean, God, please . . . (*pointing*) . . . just listen to me babbling along in there!—but I can at least say what I'm feeling, what I mean to say, and that's the truth right there. This *goddess* fell into my life in my twenty-fifth year and I never looked back. Not even once . . .

The man moves over and arranges the flowers a bit.

EDWARD . . . she was a married woman, when we met. And not like some newlywed, either, oh no. Uh-*uh*. Mary Josephine Carr—married name was Andersen—was a much-wedded lady of nineteen years and a mother of two grown boys. Indeed she was. Indeed, in-deed. (*Beat.*) Yeah, I always felt a little bad about that, me breaking up this marriage she was in. Not that she loved the guy, bastard she was with for that long—he was this Swedish businessman, first-generation American and self-made, he loved to tell you, name of *Ulrich* or some such—but this was a few years ago, *more* than a few now, and you lived with the messes you made back then. Mary Jo told me one time—and she didn't love to talk about the past, no, she did not, she was always looking forward, that woman was, toward the future—she said that she called her mother one night, right after her honeymoon, I mean, phoned her from the bridal suite at the Drake and said she'd made a mistake. That she wanted to come home, and this old bitch—excuse my directness here, but she was—Jo-Jo's mother tells her that she's made her bed now, she's gonna have to lie in it. I mean, that's her *mom* talking, so, you know—I heard that and I never felt very bad again that I grew up without any parents around! I mean, can you imagine saying that to your *own* kid? Huh? (*Beat.*) So, anyhow, that's what she did, Mary Jo. She

Neil LaBute

slept in that bed of hers for the next however many years . . .
right up until we met. Yep.

He looks around, pulls out his pack of Camels.

EDWARD   . . . and here's the bed I made for myself! A mattress
    stuffed full of tobacco leaves and tar and shit. I do apologize,
    but hey, it's the nerves and whatnot. It really is . . . (*Inhales.*)
    That's good stuff, I don't care what the doctors say, and
    believe me, they love to go on about it! Jesus, have I had to
    listen to some bullshit because of this little number right here
    . . . (*Holds up a cig.*) But I have been a faithful lover, yes I
    have. We figured out one time, just for a laugh—the kids and
    me—just how much money I'd probably dropped on cigarettes,
    I mean, on individual packs and all the cartons and stuff, over
    the years. God, it'd make your head spin . . . it really is
    unbelievable! I suppose the same could be said of the younger
    set, buying up their comic books or video games and stuff . . .
    but that junk doesn't exactly drop *cancer* in your lap, now,
    either, does it? Not yet, anyhow, but I'm sure they will discover
    some shit that's wrong with it, the scientists will, just give 'em
    some time . . . that's not all, either, the only thing these little
    babies've been responsible for, oh no. A few other near-death
    experiences that I've never discussed with the general public,
    but it's true. (*Smiles.*) I almost got Jo-Jo and me killed once
    with my smoking, yes I did. Middle of the night in . . . Iowa, I
    believe, and driving back home after being at the dedication of
    a new store in Ames. Jo, she wanted to stop at a place, just
    some cheap ol' Motel 6 or Super 8, but I felt fine, was feeling
    all good and I told her to just climb in the back and stretch out
    there—we had one of those Chrysler station wagons at the

Wrecks

time, with the faux paneling—got her to curl up on the backseat of the thing and I figure I can make it home before rush hour if I push it so I chug down a few coffees and keep the Camels burning and off we go. Cruising. (*Beat.*) Not thirty miles up the road we start getting into some dips, you know, farm country that's a little more hilly and you're going up and down through these peaks and valleys—at the bottom, in the low sides, I'm starting to hit patches of fog, this heavy sorta marsh fog that sits in these spots at night . . . burns off first thing in the morning. So I'm reaching over there into the passenger seat where I've tossed my package of smokes so I can get at 'em easier, and . . . I mean, I look away from the road for a second, a split moment there where I'm grabbing one and lighting up . . . suddenly, I've got the bat of an eye to see what's coming. There, directly in front of me, is a semi truck—this semi jackknifed across my lane of traffic and not even its flashers on. *Nothing.* Oncoming lane's got a van, one of these family minivans in it, completely flipped over and up on its roof. I don't have so much as a breath to think about it, I just let go of the wheel and throw myself sideways. We hit the thing at about sixty miles an hour and it tears the top of the car straight back, boom! Peels it like it was a tin of canned fish. I get my foot back on the brake and we go spinning around, fifty yards up the road, before I finally get us to stop. (*Beat.*) In the silence of that moment I can feel I'm alive, I know that, but I've got no idea if Jo's . . . if she's . . . you know. I'm sitting there, propped up against the steering wheel, my forehead bleeding, and all alone. One of the worst episodes of my life . . . until she sticks her head up, covered in glass and blinking—like a little baby you had to wake up from a nap—I was so goddamn happy to see that woman's

Neil LaBute

face spring up there that I . . . shit, it doesn't matter, really, but you just gotta trust me on that one. I was over the moon and then some. To see my Jo-Jo staring back at me . . . by the faintest light of our dashboard there. (*Beat.*) Young fella lost control of his vehicle, killed himself and a family of four, and that's that—a freak thing is all. It could've happened to anybody or never taken place, but it did. And we lived through it, Jo and me. Some IBM executive, all the things in life to live for, his wife and kids—and the driver, too. First month or so on the job, from all accounts happy and healthy and very glad to be pulling down a paycheck; so why are they killed and we're left sitting there and breathing life? Why did that have to happen, why are *we* untouched? Huh? I dunno, I really don't, but shit like that'll haunt you, it will, I promise you. The happenstance of life. (*Shakes his head.*) Not like what we got here, what both of us ended up facing at the prime of our destinies, with this cancer business. No, that just marches right up and rings the doorbell and says, "Guess who? Hope you don't mind but I'm staying for dinner." Diseases like this—that just keep eating at ya—they are insidious little prioks that deserve the hatred and fear we heap on 'em. They really are. Some goddamn *microbe* that does in a grown man or woman after living up into adulthood? That's bullshit is what that is! I mean it. Nothing at all you can control but you can still hate it. Yes, you can . . . *absolutely* you can! (*Beat.*) Anyway, that has nothing to do with this, what we're talking about today—and nobody, not *any*body else, knows about what I'm dealing with here so I'll ask you to keep it to yourselves—let's just forget about it and keep going, okay? Got a few other things I *need* to say, if you don't mind. Actually, even if you do, 'cause I'm not really asking your permission here and besides, I'm a widower now, so gimme a little—well, whatever it is you give a guy when his wife has passed. His *due*, I guess. Right? Gimme my due.

He smiles and stops for a moment, finishing his smoke.

EDWARD . . . I'll sit up and have one of these on the table in the morgue, if they'll let me, so just save all your little pamphlets and crap, okay? It's my life, thanks very much. At least what's left of it. Which, based on several estimates, is about eight months, give or take . . . (*Beat.*) Well, nice thing is, everybody else'll assume it was love that took me, so soon after Mary Jo. Happens to lots of older people, from what I've read or seen on the television—couples that've been together for so long, years and years like we were—when one of 'em passes on, the other's quite likely to keel over within the year. It's true. And so it'll be in this case . . . which, I suppose, is romantic in some way, when you look at it like that. Star-crossed lovers or some such. Right? And I think we were, actually, in our own way . . . or maybe just had a few *wires* crossed, that's probably more like it! "Wire-crossed" lovers, which in some sense is much more appropriate, what with our backgrounds and all. (*Beat.*) See, I met my Mary Jo through the oddest of ways, I really did. She was sitting in the back of a car, first time I saw her. Hidden way down in the enormous rear seat of a Buick Riviera, brand-new, one of those crazy-looking "boat tail" jobs they'd just come out with back in '71. Thing was *gigantic*, and I just very casually took a glance in the back—I hadn't really seen one before, on the street, I mean—and Ulrich Andersen, that guy I mentioned to you earlier, who I'm working for at the time (at one of his

Neil LaBute

warehouses), spots me as he's talking to some other men about something. *Stolen goods*, no doubt, which it was whispered that he specialized in—but he looks over and catches me by the side door, all leaning in and dumbfounded. They really are such beautiful vehicles, I don't know if you're at all familiar with 'em, but . . . well, take my word for it. His was icy white, with a ton of chrome on it and this stylish half-top of black vinyl, gorgeous. Nothing on the road like it, still isn't today. Not at all—God, don't get me started on cars or we're gonna be here all night! I mean, really . . . the absolute shit these companies get away with today and are still allowed to even use the name "automobiles" is a crime, a serious felony in my book. Every car on the road looks like a goddamn *Honda*, except for Honda, of course! No, the Japanese have moved on to some futuristic *box* with wheels stuck to it, so that's . . . it's pathetic. And not just to auto lovers like me, but for even the most casual user. Cars used to stand for something, for individuality and craftsmanship and, and . . . (*Stops.*) I sound like one of those guys, don't I? Kind you sit next to on the bus or at a diner or whatnot and you casually ask, "Hey, what time you got?" Two days later you stagger out with your life, if you're lucky! All right, I'll shut up now, at least on that particular subject. Cars.

The man pulls out another smoke, thinks about it, and puts it away.

EDWARD   . . . I can wait. Show a little willpower. Believe me, that is one thing I got plenty of. *Loads* of that stuff—which comes from being a perpetual outsider, I suppose. The foster kid, always last in line for whatever's being handed out. Yeah, I figured that one out pretty damn quick—the new boy don't count for shit, so be thankful for what you get. (*Beat.*) Sorry, must be the day or whatever, 'cause my head is spinning here—I was telling you about how Mary Jo and I met. The incident with the Buick. Yeah. (*Beat.*) *So* . . . Ulrich sees me drooling over his car there but I guess he gets it into his thick Nordic skull that I'm staring at his wife, whom I can't even really make out, thanks to the reflection off the windows, but that's not what he's thinking. No. So he shouts at me, running over in his stiff-legged European way . . . (*Imitates him.*) . . . and all up in my face, with his arms swinging and that breath of his, saying, "'Ey, Eddy, 'ey you! Boy!! Vat you doink, lookink at my vife?!!" And the guy takes a swing at me—I'm not kidding you! Not two minutes before it's a pat on the shoulder and a ten-dollar bill slipped in my pocket as he passes— I'm twenty-five years old but he treats me like a son, I didn't mind—and now he's going for my chin on a roundhouse punch. Well, look, I'm not blowing anybody's horn here, but— I grew up in twelve different houses, most of them mean shitholes, did some time in the navy, bummed around Mexico for a while—no Swedish businessman, and I don't give a damn who he is, is gonna knock me down. I step outta the way and—my whole working life passing before my eyes in a single beat, I mean, this job is putting me through *college*, after all—but I lay him out with two quick shots. One to the gut and one to that pug nose of his. Pa-pow! Down he goes. Now, of course, I proceed to get the absolute, complete, and unadulterated crap kicked outta me by most of the other fellas working in the place—on Ulrich's command—but I don't mind. It was good to see the guy drop to his knees, if only just the once. Obviously, he's insanely jealous—and I've realized that

Neil LaBute

this is true many times over since then . . . men who aren't in love with their wives are driven mad by the thought of anybody else who might be. Know what I'm saying? It's true. (*Beat.*) Actually, it's not completely clear, that story. I did see Jo-Jo's face there, just as I was blacking out. Heard some woman screaming as they were beating away on me and then this . . . *vision* . . . looking down on me as I'm drifting off. It was lovely.

He pulls out his pack of Camels and fires one up. Holds it up for all to see.

EDWARD . . . fuck it. Habit's a habit, right? That's why they call it that. (*Grins.*) Don't use that word much—"fuck"—because she always hated hearing it, my wife did, so I never said it in the house or around her if I could help it, but I see it slipping into my speech more and more these days. I gotta watch that, I do . . . there's nothing attractive about it, doesn't make you sound any tougher, it just gets to be . . . well, you know. (*Holds up his cig.*) Habit. That's all. I hear kids now, these teenagers or college boys that I hire for summer help down at the shop, sometimes saying it, and I just laugh to myself, think how stupid and silly they all sound, so I should probably practice what I preach. Fuck yes. (*Laughs.*) I'm just joking with you!

The man enjoys a nice long drag—watches the puff of smoke climb upward. Touches it with his hand.

EDWARD I guess I never mentioned what we do, huh? The little empire that Jo-Jo and I built up together, which I'm quite proud of, and which, no doubt, in eight months' time is gonna be

Wrecks

pulled to pieces by that bunch in there . . . (*He points toward the other room.*) . . . it's a string of classic auto rental stores called Carr's. Get it? Carr's Cars. Okay, yeah, kind of dopey, true, but I'm telling you now . . . people in the Midwest eat that shit up. Love it! See, the riddle was—and this came from Mary Jo—how come you can only rent *new* cars when you go somewhere? All right, that's not a riddle, exactly, more of a question, but it's asking the same basic thing. How come? Well, that's what we asked ourselves—and the answer was, because nobody out there was doing a damn thing about it! That's why. So Jo-Jo and me, and I'm not gonna lie here, with the help of the money she brought into our lives from divorcing Ulrich—seems the Swede had put a lot of his dough aside under his *wife's* name and when the time came, push come to shove, he was pretty happy to patch things up and be done with her—we started buying up all the classic automobiles we could find, from all over the U.S., bunches of these beauties that we fixed up, slapped a new coat of paint on 'em, and then started renting out to the general public. It became a *huge* deal for a while, even a small blurb about it in *Time* magazine once. Still got the clipping of it somewhere. Rent-A-Wreck, all those people . . . that idea came from us, Jo-Jo and me. One of those things, like the paper clip, probably, that just comes to you at four in the morning and you wake up a millionaire. That's how it all turned out for us—including a sale to Avis about seven years back. We still run 'em all, of course, the ones up and down the Mississippi, anyway, but we're now owned by Avis. Yeah, it all turned out real good . . . (*Beat.*) I'll tell you what, it feels pretty nice, even still, I can be driving through the center of town or out on the highway— happened to me just last week—and I had a '65 Impala, blue

Neil LaBute

with a white top, and the original 327 in it, roar past me with this, oh, probably thirty-five-year-old businessman sitting up front, talking on his cell and no doubt headed to a meeting somewhere. Back license plate holder is one of ours—says, "I may be old, but I'm ahead of you!" I thought that up and it kills me. I love that! Then, underneath, it states, "I got it at Carr's Cars." With the 800 number. It makes you proud, you know? When you've done something like that, created something. (*Looks at the others again.*) Hope to God they can keep it together after I'm gone and not be at each other's throats down at the city gates. Be a shame to have our little kingdom wither away over some petty shit like who's gonna be in charge or that type of thing. But, hey, you all know how families can be . . . most unloving creatures that the good Lord ever collected together in one place, what you often come to find out. In situations like this, anyhow. Death does strange stuff to folks, and that's no big mystery I'm unveiling there. (*Beat.*) Somebody dies, you line up the next of kin on either side of all the valuables and just watch 'em go at it. Tells you a whole bunch about humanity, right there. Worse than seeing a *pro wrestling* match, that's what that is! Yeah, glad I'm gonna miss it when her boys start tearing into each other. (*Beat.*) See, it's not my girls, no, they'd never . . . it's her sons. From the first marriage. *Them.*

The man waves this notion off—finishes his cigarette.

EDWARD I know I'm leaving a lot out here but you'll just have to believe me on this—I told you the highlights 'cause lots of that stuff is . . . private, and that's fine with me, it is, that's *okay*—it's private for a reason. But yes, we had an affair, I believe I've already mentioned that—the part I'm not too proud of—but that marriage of hers was long over by this point. Really, just painting by numbers when we first started seeing each other. I'm serious. I wouldn't go and ruin the lives of some kids like that if the thing was . . . trust me on that little point. I've been privy to far too much of that particular brand of shit to also be a party to it, so no. But I see her again, like five months later, I mean, after the run-in with Ulrich, at this soiree—with Mary Jo in the most luminous lavender-colored dress and these elegant brooches holding it on over each shoulder—my God, now this was a woman! She was . . . unnerving. I'm not kidding you, that's what she was. Made me feel like some baby boy, all nervous and everything inside. But that's how it started, now you know—lots of gossip and shouting matches with ol' Ulrich and things that I don't even know how Mary Jo ever made it through, because she was always such a fragile woman—it started that way. With me spotting her in that dress as she entered the ballroom in a mansion up in Kenilworth. (*Beat.*) I was at the thing by a fluke—a guy who owned the place, his son I knew from night school and he'd invited me up for the weekend and it happened to coincide with this big party his old man was throwing—anyway, I walked right up to her, in my jeans and a borrowed jacket, and said, "Hello again." Reminded her of the time we first met, and I don't think a day went by, literally from that second on, that we didn't spend time together, on the phone or in person or something. And this was all way before your Internet or cell phones or anything of the sort—we managed it because we were in love, not because it was easy. Today you like some gal or, hey, you're not even sure, what's it take to dial her up, track her down, ask her out? Send her an

Neil LaBute

e-mail? About a minute. Maybe less. But in my day—God, now I know I'm old and dying, "my day"!—if you wanted something, you had to work for it. And that's what Jo-Jo and I did. We both worked on our relationship every day of our lives, thick and thin, richer and poorer and, well, obviously, the health stuff, too . . . we never gave up on each other. Not one time. (*Beat.*) Doesn't mean I didn't sleep on the couch a few nights, but shit . . . I didn't move out because of it! People today are so . . . you know. Everybody's all ready to take offense. Pack it in. Give it up. I don't understand this world anymore, I truly do not. Might just be a good thing that I'm outta here pretty soon, because I am starting to feel like an alien life force more and more. When I had a goal, I stuck with it—stuck in there for *years* until I'd reach it! Like a pit bull or something, one of those snapping turtles, hanging on to a stick long after it was dead. That was me. Guess it comes with the . . . you know, territory. (*Beat.*) You grow up like one of those characters in some *Charles Dickens* book and you'll know what I'm saying. You get a thing in your head that you want and you hold on to it, at all cost. You *hold* on. And that's what I did with my Mary Jo. I finally got her and I hold on to her right up until the last minute of her life . . . in my arms and me staring down into her sweet, sweet face. That's what I did, thank you very much. I did indeed.

He starts to move away but suddenly turns in a tight circle, looking back around at us.

EDWARD   . . . and you know why? Any idea how come I was obsessed with Mary Jo in this way? Huh? Because she was *worth* loving, that's why. Yeah. And you can't say that about

everybody you run into on the street, not any longer . . .
But she was. She was like a woman haunted, looking for
something out there on the horizon—you could see it in her
eyes—and when she found a thing like love, real, true love
like we offered each other . . . well, she would cling to it like
wreckage from an airplane gone missing out over the ocean.
When we met, middle of this fancy-dress party, she saw that
in me. She did. That I was worth holding on to. And for me,
hell, listen—I spent my whole life looking for her. Right up until
that moment. All those things I mentioned before—armed
services, my travel—I never touched a woman before her, no, I
didn't and I don't give two shits if you believe me or not—but
I never did. Sure, kisses and the like, *second base*, maybe,
but never once did I lie in bed with a woman in that way—the
biblical way is what I'm referring to here, for the slower ones
in the group—until Mary Jo and I slept together on the first
night of our marriage. Course it was different then, a complete
and utterly different age than we have here now, and I'd
consider it a golden one, too. I really would. Filled with some
chivalry and proper thoughts and holding the door open for a
lady, which gets you nothing but a strange look and maybe
even the *finger* these days, I kid you not. Honestly, fifteen-
year-old girl flipped me off once, I held the door for her at a
restaurant! What's it all coming to, I ask you? (*Shakes his
head and crosses to the casket.*) I guess this now would be
the equivalent of one of those videos I mentioned before,
because what I'm gonna tell you here about us, well . . . I just
don't do that. Normally, I mean. Never have, and I'm including
my friends and drinking buddies, all that. Many times as guys
pumped me for info about Jo-Jo, I didn't ever tell stories out of
school. What's private is private, but God, lemme tell you—I

Neil LaBute

couldn't get enough of her. Just couldn't! Her skin, the sight of her body, the feel of that . . . to be in her, inside of Mary Jo, was like choir music, seriously—I used to almost pass out and could see bright lights, hear music, all sorts of shit when we'd make love. It was out of this world and that's where our kids come from . . . (*He points at the others.*) . . . directly out of all that bliss. Not that I don't love children, because I do, absolutely do, but I'm not gonna make things up for you. They're with us today because of one thing only: I loved having sex with their mother. I really did. It almost frightened me sometimes, both of us, I think, how great it felt. And it never waned for me, it didn't, in any way, all through our life, right up until—well, not too long before what we found out. About Mary Jo and her sickness there . . . (*Beat.*) No Viagra, either, none of that *chemical* bullshit that folks need to go through today, uh-uh—she was all I ever needed, Jo-Jo was. (*He touches at his pants.*) God, that's embarrassing! Huh? Didn't expect *that* to happen . . . not here, anyway. But, see, that's what I'm saying about her . . . even now when she's gone. I love her, goddamnit! So, so much.

He stops and listens for a moment. Checks his watch.

EDWARD We're wrapping up in there now, so I s'pose I better get back to it. Try and say my good-byes and all that . . . and I'm not just saying that because of what happened there, I'm not. It's . . . whatever. I'm too old to get embarrassed, and I got nothing to be ashamed of, I can tell you that much. Not one thing when it comes to Mary Jo . . .

He turns to go, then swings around. Looks out again.

Wrecks

EDWARD . . . she didn't deserve what she got, I'll say that one final thing and then I'll go. All right? She did not. (*Beat.*) Me smoking like a Christmas stove all my life and she's the one who goes and gets cancer! That's like some sick joke that you hear in a men's magazine, that's what that is. I mean, yeah, I got it *now*, but at the time . . . I just couldn't wrap my head around it. Neither one of us could, which is the way the universe likes to play it sometimes, at least from what I've seen. God likes it that way just fine, thank you very much . . . Keeping us guessing. (*Beat.*) I gotta say, though, when I got the news, I was, I don't know, almost . . . elated, I suppose. And that probably sounds, I know, but lemme explain . . . see, when I heard that, when she rang me down at the office and told me, asked me to come home, all on the drive there I was, like, *beaming* inside because now—and I knew it was bad, she told me that much about the results—*now* I was certain that I'd be able to be there with her, every day, for the rest of her life. And that excited me somehow. (*Beat.*) 'Cause, see, all during our marriage, from the moment we stepped off the *altar*, practically, I had a terrible sense that I wouldn't be there when she died. Just some premonition or something, this feeling, and it used to spook the shit outta me. Honestly, I used to fear going out on business trips; even when we were negotiating the whole Avis deal I hated being away from home. From her. And not just because I missed her, because I would, horribly, but also because I had that weird sensation that she might be taken away from me somehow. A hit-and-run or whatever, when I wasn't there. Made for some long nights spent in hotel rooms and a lotta long-distance calls, believe you me! Oh, well, I loved hearing her voice like that, at night, as I was drifting off. It was terrific . . .

The man wavers now, unsure whether to go on.

EDWARD . . . not much to say about her death, really. Not much
and *volumes*, I guess. She faced it like some old-time hero or
something, quite honestly, out of a book of myths—never
before have I seen a person leave this earth in such a
dignified way. Ever. Period, and I did a little time in Southeast
Asia and that sort of deal, if you know what I mean, so . . .
I've seen my share of it. Hope to Christ I do it with the same
sorta grace, but I doubt it. Somehow I doubt it . . . (*Beat.*)
Anyway, nobody likes hearing that shit, right? I mean the grisly
day-to-day of it, unless you're going through it, maybe, or
you're just perverted and a weirdo, so I'll skip a bit of that,
but . . . her last day, Tuesday, that she left us on . . . couldn't
have·been more perfect. The weather, I mean. All weekend
had been pissing down rain, absolute buckets, and Monday,
too, really, but that Tuesday broke with a beautiful sunrise,
which she could see from her bed—Jo-Jo demanded that we
do this at home, let her finish off there and not in some
goddamn hospital room and I agreed, although the boys fought
me even on that point, even on *that*—she was lying there,
nurse was downstairs, taking a coffee break, and I was alone
with her—kids were all still sleeping or at their hotels and not
back at the house yet—and she . . . you know, she just let go.
It was time for it and she was, I mean, completely lucid and
she just . . . slipped off. Away. It'd been a hell of a battle and
I was glad to have done with it, quite truthfully. To watch
someone you love do that, put up that kind of struggle, hour
after hour . . . I just wanted her to be at peace, you know? To
dream and not have to, well, whatever. Nobody can put that
shit into words, and especially not me . . . (*Beat.*) Before she

went, I mean, just a few moments before, she . . . Mary Jo took my hand and smiled at me, this perfectly serene smile—not the frightened look of a person about to die, not even that look that she sometimes had in her eyes, that I told you about—she smiled up at me, so sweetly, and whispered that she had a thing to tell me. A secret. Something she'd never told anyone, all her life, and that she needed to say to me, to tell the man she loved . . . (*Beat.*) And she did. Whispered it in my ear and was gone a minute or so later, but for that time, those sixty or so seconds, I could see a lifetime drop away. This mantle that she'd been . . . It's just amazing what we do, as people, you know, to run from the past. Isn't it? God, the *swamplands* we're willing to wade through to get around truth! It just floors me. She told me that—her secret—and I leaned down and kissed her, right there, on the lips. Fully on the lips and whispered back to her. Four words and then that look on her face. Not of death or fear or anything else but pure relief. Absolute freedom. Yeah. It was a beautiful day . . .

The man pulls out the cigarettes again—final one in the pack. He fires it up.

EDWARD . . . last one, I promise. I finish this and I'll shut my big mouth. So look, I'm not gonna tell you what I said to her, so don't go asking. It's between Jo-Jo and me, private, and I choose not to. I'm sure Mary Jo wouldn't care if I told you what she whispered to me, however, because once she voiced it, had finally got it out . . . well, she was free of it. Released. (*Beat.*) You have to understand the time, what this dates back to. As I said, I'm a different generation and she was a lot

Neil LaBute

older than *me*, so you can imagine the . . . it goes back to her mom. Yeah, the old bat I mentioned before with the "lie in your own bed" shit. Her. See, Mary Jo, years before any of us knew her, and I'm talking about every person there in that crowd . . . (*Points.*) . . . she had a kid. Got pregnant by a visiting uncle, from the sound of it—the *mother's* brother, of course—and was sent away. Off to have the baby in some out-of-the-way family home—they were quite wealthy, I believe—and then gave that child away. Left it to the state or however people did it then—even having gone through it, I'm no authority. Left it on a doorstep or down at the church, I don't know. But that was the thing she'd done, her big *crime* that she carried around in her heart all this time—some pig of a man had raped her and she was to blame. That was the bed she made for herself, I guess, and so when she couldn't take it anymore, the shit that her mother threw at her, day after day . . . well, she ran off and married the first guy who came along who had so much as a clean shave and a smile on his face. Ulrich Andersen. And we all know how that turned out. (*Beat.*) But through it all, the years with Ulrich and what we went through together and having more kids, even at her late age, right up until the cancer—you never saw a more gracious and loving person walking the lanes and fields of this great country of ours. No, you did not. And that, my friends, is what makes Mary Josephine Delaney Andersen Carr so worth remembering. At a time and in a country where the past hardly seems to count for two shakes of a stick dipped in shit . . . she is *worth* noting because . . . well, if you didn't get it from all I've just said, then I don't really care if you remember her or not. Indeed I *don't*.

He finishes off the smoke and stubs it out. Waits.

EDWARD . . . but hey, her little secret's safe with me. It is. Safe
for now, and my "now" isn't gonna be a hell of a lot longer,
so . . . yeah. (*Indicates.*) I'd never tell that bunch over there,
ever, not even my own flesh and blood, because they wouldn't
understand and they'd bitch and moan and be terrified of it,
turn a blind eye to the truth. The truth about somebody they're
supposed to care for. I mean, Jesus God in heaven, how did
we ever get to a place like that? And I mean any of us. Huh?
Where we can't bear to hear the truth anymore. We cringe in
the shadows and weep if a person tells it like it is. Better to
just go along, lying to ourselves and each other, big smiles
plastered on our faces at our kid's soccer games or at the
mall and just hope we make it to the end . . . (*Holds up his
hands.*) . . . to this place, here, without our neighbors
guessing what's really going on inside our heads. Ho-ly shit.
Well, like I said before, we're an odd group, we are. A regular
bunch of misfits. (*Beat.*) Nah, I'm not gonna tell them shit, or
anyone else for that matter, because of how they'd react or
the plain simple fact that it's none of their business—most
people, I mean. It's none of their affair. Doesn't mean I'm
ashamed of it or trying to hide it, but just . . . you know what
I'm saying. Fact of the deal is, the heart of this particular
matter—I always knew she had a secret. My Mary Jo. I did.
Knew that's what was going on deep down in those golden
eyes of hers, way, way back inside . . . that she was carrying
something else around. I knew it because—well, maybe you're
all a bunch smarter than I take you for—*I* was her secret. Me.
(*Beat.*) 'Member I said that once I had an idea of what I
wanted in this life that I went after it? Held on to it? Well, she

Neil LaBute

was it. Jo-Jo was my reason for living. I guess I figured, I
mean—not that I have to justify it to any of you because,
believe me, I don't, but—I suppose once I found her, knew her
name and all, I'm saying . . . I figured if she didn't want me in
one way, in that way . . . as her kid . . . then maybe it'd be
able to work out for us in some different life. A life like we've
had together. And I was right, I was completely true about
that! It was . . . well, I'm sick of trying to explain, so accept it
or not, but I'm telling you—we had ourselves an amazing time
together. But, yeah, I did always know who she was. And that
her "staring out to sea"—that's what I used to call it—that it
was for me. *About* me. (*Beat.*) Took a long time to gather
that info, trust me, lots of letters and begging and shit, and
this again was a time before the information highway came
roaring up our collective asses, this was back in the days of
microfiche and "I'm sorry but I can't help you" and if a person
didn't wanna be found it was hard as shit to find 'em. (*Beat.*)
I dated a girl—this little redhead back in Idaho—for a year
and a half, eighteen *months*, just to get my mother's maiden
name. Lucky for me she was a good churchgoing girl and we
didn't take it too far but I had to promise her the moon,
anyway, even then. Broke off our engagement and skipped
town the day after she came to my place with the mimeograph
of my birth certificate . . . So, no, I'm not proud of everything
I did along the way. But hey . . . what's done is done.
Indeed it is. (*Beat.*) It wasn't easy after that, either, believe
me . . . no cakewalk just having her name. It was years and
years of wandering about, dead ends and all the rest . . .
yes, it was. *Yes.* But I did it. Oh yeah, I finally did do it. Found
my way here. Home. To her. My Mary Jo. (*A moment.*) My
mom . . .

The man smiles and heads off. He turns a final time.

EDWARD . . . I just want you to know, though, to realize that it was
worth it to me. All of this I did, what might conventionally
be thought of as "wrong" or at least well off "the beaten
track" . . . I wouldn't change a minute of it. Not a single
second. To be loved is never wrong, or to love a person, like I
did, how I've done. I spent my *lifetime*—the only one God gave
me—making a woman happy and she did the same for me
and not one fly or blade of grass ever suffered because of it—
not *one*. Now . . . how many of you can say the same? (*Beat.*)
I'll tell you what . . . love's a pretty special creature, no matter
what form it comes in. I honestly believe that . . . I do.

He turns and looks at the portrait of his mother. Remembering.

*Sound of the others in the next room—talking. Music slowly
rising.*

Silence. Darkness.

Neil LaBute

Liars Club

Production History

Liars Club had its first production on February 24, 2002, as part of the 24 Hour Plays at the Henry Fonda Theater in Los Angeles. Director: Neil Pepe.

ACTOR NO. 1   Clark Gregg

ACTOR NO. 2   Devon Gummersall

ACTRESS NO. 1   Portia de Rossi

ACTRESS NO. 2   Brooke Smith

Characters

FOUR ACTORS—ages vary

Setting

A bare stage

Silence. Darkness.

Four spots appear onstage in an even row. Another one a bit farther down in blue. Dim at first, the four brighten as a performer steps into each. After a moment, four actors (two MEN *and two* WOMEN*) stare back at the audience.*

Finally, one of the actors steps forward into the blue spot and begins to speak.

ACTOR NO. 1 Hi, good evening, how's it going? Great . . . that's great. Yes. I'm ——— and it's really nice to be here tonight, doing the show and all that. Seriously. Good cause and whatever . . . This is a benefit, right? I think so . . . yeah, it is. Course it is. Otherwise I'd be getting *paid*. (*Beat.*) So, lemme tell you how this is gonna go, just lay out a little, ahhh, groundwork for you and we'll get moving. 'Kay?

He gestures to both sides, taking in the other performers as he speaks out front.

ACTOR NO. 1 All right . . . so, you know how this whole thing works, correct? How the evening's been running—so we figured that . . . we *decided* along with our writer . . . to do things just a little bit differently. Add in some audience participation and that type of deal. Blah-blah-blah. Okay, so what *we've* created here, I mean, our writer did . . . (*Stops and thinks.*) He said that we'd, umm . . . wait, now *I'm* confused . . .

Liars Club

ACTOR NO. 2 Come on, man, just do it . . .

ACTRESS NO. 1 We only have twenty minutes.

ACTOR NO. 1 Right, right, sorry . . . (*to audience*) He said that we'd, ahhh . . .

ACTRESS NO. 2 Let's go, hurry up!

ACTOR NO. 1 I will, I'm sorry, I blanked there for a second! Haven't been onstage in a while . . . (*to audience*) I'm on a *series*.

ACTRESS NO. 2 You want me to finish it? I mean, explaining . . . I will.

ACTOR NO. 1 Seriously? That'd be great. Completely. Ladies and gentlemen, ———!

ACTOR NO. 1 *steps back into position as* ACTRESS NO. 2 *moves forward into the blue.*

ACTRESS NO. 2 Hey, hello, sorry about that. Time's precious, okay, that's why we're all feeling . . . anyway. So what we decided to do here is—and I think it's kind of a fun idea—is to blend reality and illusion a bit tonight. Fact and fiction. Truth. Untruth. Make some drama out of our own lives and see what you think . . .

ACTRESS NO. 1 Sort of a Mike Leigh thing . . .

ACTOR NO. 2 Or like Cassavetes . . . but without all the handheld shit.

ACTRESS NO. 2 Hey, guys, come on . . . *I'm* doing it, all right? Those are both movie references, anyway, not theater. (*to audience*) It's more like Pirandello or somebody like that . . .

ACTRESS NO. 1 Yeah. Sort of a Samuel Beckett thing . . .

ACTOR NO. 2 Or like Ionesco . . . but without all the handheld shit.

ACTRESS NO. 2 Would you stop with the . . . ?!

ACTOR NO. 2 Sorry.

ACTOR NO. 1 You know, *I* could've explained it *this* badly . . .

ACTRESS NO. 2 That's true . . . (*back to audience*) All right, look, I'll
do it fast and we'll get started. Basically, it's more like "reality
TV" than anything else, I mean, if you were gonna *compare* it
to something—but it's still theater, it's *absolutely* theater. It
is. See, the writer of this piece thought it'd be a cool idea to
take a real-life thing from each of our pasts, like, a . . . well,
just some moment that was, ummm . . .

ACTOR NO. 1 You know . . . basically, a "bad" moment.

ACTOR NO. 2 Yeah, the embarrassing shit.

ACTRESS NO. 2 Right, yes, thank you . . . a less than savory
incident from our histories . . . like, before we became,
well . . . whoever we are now. So he takes these little
episodes and fabricates them a bit, alters the sexes, even,
and then we're each supposed to, ahhh . . .

ACTRESS NO. 1 Wait. Not each of us, you said "each" and that's . . .

ACTRESS NO. 2 Sorry, no, that's not . . . see, I wasn't the one
originally picked to do the intro for a reason! (*Smiles.*) Okay,
look, he took three of these stories from our lives,
embellished them a bit, and then gave the new scripted
versions back to us, each to a person other than the one it
happened to. (*Beat.*) Follow me? 'S not too confusing, right?
Okay . . .

ACTOR NO. 1 Yeah, but tell 'em the other part . . .

ACTOR NO. 2 The *good* part. The fakey bit . . .

ACTRESS NO. 2 I am, I'm getting there, Jesus! All right, so three
parts are real but added to, and the fourth part he totally
made up and gave to the last actor. Only stipulation is that
you can't be telling your own story. And so, I mean, that's it.
Picked at random out of a hat and off we go. Seriously, we
even used a hat . . . (*Beat.*) You guys listen to us tonight, let

us speak, and try to figure out who's telling the lie. It's like . . . improv meets a game show meets one of those horrible profile things on the E! channel . . . Sort of a *What's My Line?* deal . . . (*looking around*) Or *Liar's Club.* 'Member that one, from the '70s?

ACTOR NO. 2 Kinda like Springer. But without the handheld shit . . .

ACTRESS NO. 2 Exactly! And nobody fat takes their shirt off. So . . . (*To audience.*) Rather than some lame comedy revue, we thought we'd actually do a little dramatic mind-fuck and see how that goes . . .

ACTOR NO. 2 Yeah. People say actors never *really* give anything back to the audience. Well, now they're gonna be sorry . . . (*offstage*) We ready? Let's go . . .

ACTRESS NO. 2 *abruptly returns to her spot and lights dim to the single bright blue spot.* ACTOR NO. 2 *steps into it and begins.*

ACTOR NO. 2 All right, so I'm first. Fine. Good. (*to audience*) My name is ———, I'm an actor, and the story you're about to hear is totally true, I mean, it happened. I was maybe sixteen—around there, anyway—and I met this person at school. Beautiful, wonderful, first-love kind of thing. And we start going out, just movies and stuff at first but definitely getting more into it really quick. Bing-bang, and a month or so later, I find out a really hard truth. I'm pregnant . . . (*Laughs.*) Okay, sorry, I had to do that . . . but it really would've sucked, wouldn't it, I mean for me, if I'd picked something like that! All right, here I go, this is it . . . and this is totally true. (*Beat.*) I fucked someone once, I mean "mouth" fucked, one time. Without their permission . . . well, while they were *asleep.*

Neil LaBute

A babysitter who was over at our house—this was around Christmas vacation of my junior year at school—and my parents are out at this party, one of those holiday parties for my dad's work or something. Gonna be back after midnight and I'm not due home until the next morning but I made really good time. Driving in from Colorado. I had one of those VW vans, which was all over the road in the snow but I still did okay. Anyhow, this sitter—boy or girl, I won't say which—was over and supposed to be watching my little brother and sister but had passed out in the family room. *Barney Miller* is running on the tube and she/he looks to have had about ten or twelve hits off the ol' eggnog deluxe that Dad has tucked away in the fridge. Completely out and my baby sister is crying and soaked when I walk in the door. Well, I look at the scene for about half a second, head upstairs to the nursery, change her, and walk straight back down to the couch and pry open this kid's lips. Start jacking off right there, banging up against his or her teeth and pop their mouth open at the final second and give 'em one last cup a holiday cheer for the road. They didn't even stir . . . not a bit. I zipped up and headed upstairs with my bags and jumped into the sack. About twenty minutes later my folks pull in, I hear all the chatter and I do the "sleepy-eye" thing, come downstairs in my sweats and all "Hey, hi, what's going on?" Dad's so wasted that I offer to drive her/him home and we talk about our high school all the way to their place. Only when a car passes me from time to time can I see her/him kind of licking their lips, wondering why that eggnog had such a "kick" . . . We get to their place, I wish 'em merry Christmas, and that, I'm afraid, is that. (*Beat.*) And that's totally true.

ACTOR NO. 2 *steps back into place and* ACTRESS NO. 2 *steps into the blue.*

ACTRESS NO. 2 Hello again, I'm ———, and I'm gonna tell you a quick story and then you can try to figure it out . . . not that it happened to me, you know, we already discussed how this all works but I just wanna be clear about that . . . your job is not to work out whose story is whose—that would be sort of embarrassing, actually!—but to try and decide which one of these things is made up. Just thought I should, I mean, whatever. (*Beat.*) Okay, this is totally true. I mean it . . . I once washed an old lady's hair whom I was supposed to be taking care of with a cup of my own pee. I did. Not like a full glass or anything, but just one of those little Dixie cup jobs that they had at the hospital that I worked at. See, what happened was, she was a teacher of mine, from elementary school, and so she must've been, oh, what, maybe close to eighty, eighty-five when I ran into her at the nursing home. At least that. She was a total bitch—excuse me, but she was—when I was in first grade. The hit-your-hands-with-a-pointer kind of lady who absolutely terrorized all the kids in my class. Completely. I mean, this one time, during winter, she made the boys who got their pants wet at recess, she made them wear this old skirt of hers at their desks. Really! Or if you peed yourself by accident, anything, you had to put your pants up on the heater and sit in your underwear for an hour or so. Lose all your daily privileges. Totally traumatic sort of woman! And years later, like I said, she's placed into care where I'm working by her two daughters because she's delusional, Alzheimer's and all, and they can't take care of her or don't want to or something.

They never visited her after that, not that I saw, so it was probably the other. The "don't want to" scenario. Which was kind of sad, I suppose, but hey, she earned it, I'm sure. (*Beat.*) Anyhow, I only work on her floor one time, just once because I'm getting ready to give up the job for a nighttime position so I can audition during the day . . . and I'm assigned to get her ready for bed. Fine, whatever, I can do it. I tell 'em "fine." Now, it's a Tuesday, so it's pretty dead, people taking baths, watching TV and such, and so I get her in the bathroom of her sleeping area, hidden off behind this wall, and I make her strip. Which she does without a problem, big smile at me as she goes, she's suddenly like a pussycat since they brought her in. And there she sits—buck naked, edge of the tub, mouth moving a bit and smiling. So I open my pants and take down one of the little cups out of the dispenser, show her what I'm doing as I squat to fill it up . . . and then I pour it all over her head. Not fast, or slow, or anything. I just let it run down through her hair and onto her shoulders. Dripping onto the floor. I work it into her hair slowly, like it's full of rich lather, and then let her sit there in it for a moment. Take it all in. It's only a single look that betrays her in the end, 'cause she's still smiling and everything at the same time, but her eyes uncloud briefly and at that moment I see it. The truth. That somewhere inside, inside all that fog and despair and uncertainty, she knows what I was doing. (*Beat.*) After, I weave my way back down the hall to the nurses' station and ask everybody, "Hey, have you seen Miss Morby anywhere? I just washed her hair . . ." and we all go looking, find her just how I left her. Naked and covered in piss. I do a little dance, talk about disrespect and that I'm sure she did it on purpose.

Short version is, I pay her back for fucking up my childhood and she loses house privileges for a week. Which was a long time coming, but very sweet. (*Beat.*) And that is totally true.

ACTRESS NO. 2 *steps back into place and* ACTOR NO. 1 *steps into the blue.*

ACTOR NO. 1 Okay, this is . . . I'm just gonna go for it, get it done, because I don't really like this story, it's not mine, and I wanna finish, so let's go. I'm ———, remember? ———, and this is totally true. This story. (*Beat.*) I killed a man once. I did. Well, not killed him exactly, but got him killed, which is pretty much the same thing, right? Basically. Yeah . . . so I'm at a 7-Eleven, this is in Chicago about seven or eight years ago, around the Rogers Park area, and it's late, like, one-thirty or so, and I stop in for a pack of cigarettes, maybe a chocolate milk. I've been out with my friends and I'm heading home to this person I'm living with who stayed in bed because of the flu. Follow me so far? Great. Anyway, I decide, hey, I've been drinking, I better get a pack of gum, too, freshen the breath while I'm at it, only here's the thing: I don't have enough cash for the gum. Only another, like, eighty-five cents, but I don't have it! So . . . I get the guy talking for ten, fifteen minutes, the cashier guy, while I slowly slide a packet of Big Red up my sleeve. I do. Just keep inching toward it until I've got the thing tucked away. After, I thank the guy for staying open—he's like two seconds from closing down when I show up—and slip out with my smokes, the choco drink, and my gum. I hold the door open for two schoolkids as I go, probably trying to get a six-pack or something without getting carded. Through the glass, the dude at the register looks at me, like, "Hey, man, thanks a lot!" and after he did me the favor and let me in. I just smile and shrug, take off across the parking lot. Fast-forward to morning. I'm in the middle of a little early a.m. love—my partner is obviously feeling much better, that's the great thing about the flu, it passes—so I'm doing it, right, from behind but kind of watching the TV as we go. In the mirror. No big deal, I always do that! Keeps us close and me up-to-date on news and weather . . . anyhow, I see the guy's face flash up on the screen for a second, this black cashier guy, and then this shot of his store all police-taped off. Two teenagers have been arrested, they said, for killing the owner of the joint as he was closing down for the night. They took a package of Hostess Ding Dongs and twenty-*six* dollars from the till. It's right about then that it starts to hit me, I mean, the meaning of the thing, just as I'm about to cum. I'm kneeling there, getting ready to release, and this man's face is on the tube again and I can see the package of gum on the end table there and I just start crying. I do. I burst out bawling as I climax and I just lie there after, holding my lover and blubbering like a *two*-year-old. I mean, shit . . . you know? I don't know what to say later, have no idea, so I tell 'em, my live-in, that it was amazing and that I was just feeling really close to them right at that moment and that's why the tears. (*Beat.*) We both fall off to sleep a little while later . . . Actually, they sleep and I stare at the ceiling for a long time but you get the idea . . . and that's totally true. It is . . .

ACTOR NO. 1 *finishes up and walks back to his white spot.* ACTRESS NO. 1 *steps up next.*

ACTRESS NO. 1 Hi, I'm ———, and what I'm about to tell you is totally true. Not only that, but it's still happening, right now, as

we speak. Umm, okay, where should I begin? Let's see . . .
I have a problem. Big problem. I keep trying to get this person
I've been seeing to understand that I'm . . . (*She stops,
thinks.*) No, fuck it, you know what? You're here, right now,
let's just get to the bottom of it, front of everybody, I don't
care. I'm not gonna stand up here and do the "friend of a
friend" routine when we can just . . . so here we go. (*pointing*)
Don't try and scrunch down, I can see you, right there! So
listen to me . . .

ACTRESS NO. 1 *catches herself, thinks about it, then plunges on.*

ACTRESS NO. 1 . . . I'm curious, I wanna know, what is it? What is
bothering you, I mean, what *specific* part of it really gets you?
Hmm? The fact that I'm fucking somebody, or that the
somebody was him? Somebody you know. (*Beat.*) Funny thing
is, you used to talk to me like that—whisper to me, ask who
else I'd like to be fucking, if it wasn't you. Do you remember
that? When we first got together. You'd be on top of me and
holding me—not down exactly, but kind of like that—pinning
me and talking all that in my ear. Do you remember? And you
wanted to know, you really did want to, I'm not sure why . . .
guys just do shit like that, I guess. You wanted to see if I
would, I suppose . . . ever fuck anyone else. I mean, you
must've needed to prove it, or disprove it to yourself, or
maybe you just wanted to watch and take pictures. I dunno.
Something. Over and over you used to say that, like it was
your mantra . . . 'member? "Who else, who else, who would it
be? Who?" Again and again. Even throwing out the names of
people we both knew, guys from around town or wherever.
(*Smiles.*) So . . . I guess it just stuck, huh? And now that I've

Neil LaBute

done it, I mean, really, really fucked someone—fucked 'em good!—you're a bit broken up about it, aren't you? But why? Hmm? I don't get it . . . because you know 'em, because he's a buddy from work, or just because you're a guy and you're worried that the story's gonna get out? Well don't, it's safe with me . . . I just fucked 'em, you're the one who *likes* 'em. I just did it because I like fucking . . . not him or you or anyone, really, I just like doing it. Fucking. I really do. And I realized it, just, like, the other day; I was in Starbucks or Wal-Mart or somewhere, looking for some change, I think, and I stopped dead there. Stopped and had to get out of line, catch my breath because it did sorta just come to me. I'm *totally* into fucking, I am, and I had kinda given it up. For you. Stopped it so that you could have this normal kind of relationship thing that you say your parents never had—I mean, neither did mine but that's okay—and you really seemed to need the stability so I thought, what the hell, okay, and we moved into your place and we sleep together and every so often you go down on me, like, as a sort of monthly exchange of services, I guess, and that's that, I suppose, right? I should be happy with whatever you throw my way. But, see, I was there in that place—maybe it was the movie theater—and I was just sorta moved by the whole idea that, like, wow, you know what? Fuck this, I like spreading my legs and giving head and all that shit that you just don't seem to get into. And I like us, I think we're pretty okay together and we should see where this thing goes, but I enjoy that other shit too and I'm gonna do it and if it makes you or my mom or whoever the hell it is blush, then you better run out and buy some *powder*, 'cause I really have no plans for stopping. Not right now, and not this summer, or because nice people don't do that. And if that's the case, that it's not Christian, or decent or right . . . then fuck it all. Everything. *Especially* me! I love getting fucked, I love me, and right now that's all I'm into. *Me.* And by the way, I wouldn't dwell too long on the "how could this happen?" aspect of things . . . I never said that this was the first time. I said it was the first time you caught me. (*Smiles.*) Wow . . . I bet this is more than you bargained for tonight, huh? Sorry, honey. (*deep breath, then to the audience*) And that, as the guy right there knows . . . (*pointing*) . . . is totally true.

ACTRESS NO. 1 *steps back and* ACTOR NO. 1 *steps forward again.*

ACTOR NO. 1 Okay, that's everybody. Great! (*to where* ACTRESS NO. 1 *pointed*) Ouch, sorry, man . . . (*back to audience*) Well . . . you've heard us out, got the stories in your heads, and now we'll have a quick vote . . . who is the liar among us? Is it (*hand above his head*) me? Applaud for your choice, that's probably the easiest way . . . so, me? No? Okay . . . is it ———? (*Waits.*) Or ———? (*Waits.*) Or is it ———? Which? (*back to the other actors*) Will the real "liar" please step forward? I said, Liar, please step into the center now . . .

Each actor does a false start in turn, like the old game show, then joins ACTOR NO. 1 *onstage. Long pause. Finally,* ACTRESS NO. 1 *steps out into the blue spot. The others join in around her.*

ACTOR NO. 1 ———, ladies and gentlemen! Our big, fat liar for the night! Well, not *fat*, but you know what I'm saying . . . (*Laughs.*) If you voted for her, then you are pretty damn clever and saw right through our little ruse this evening, so give yourselves a round of applause! (*He waits.*) Good for you! And thanks again, one and all, for indulging us and being such good sports. As ever, we in the performance industry exist to serve and entertain you and I, speaking for all my fellow thespians—as uncomfortable as that word makes me!—we sincerely hope that we've done that for you here tonight . . . so thank you and good evening.

The performers join hands now and wait for applause. A set of two deep bows. They smile and start off, but ACTOR NO. 2 *stops and looks back. The others follow.*

ACTOR NO. 2 Dude, you should say something . . .

ACTRESS NO. 1 Seriously . . .

ACTOR NO. 1 Yeah?

ACTRESS NO. 2 Why not? Go ahead . . .

ACTOR NO. 1 Cool . . . (*Beat.*) Oh, man, no . . . that's . . . (*to* ACTRESS NO. 2) You do it.

ACTRESS NO. 2 Fine . . . (*Turns to the audience.*) Folks, gotta be upfront with you now. You were all wrong, actually. We just made that last little bit up, the whole "it was her" part. Y'all been screwed! (*She smiles.*) And not just because you're slow or didn't listen well enough or anything like that—but because everything that we told you was made up. Lies. Our writer created a bunch of bullshit and you believed it because, well, basically, because we're actors. Great actors . . . we *made* you believe it.

ACTRESS NO. 1 None of the stories were true. Not a single word . . .

ACTOR NO. 2 You listened and speculated and clapped because you wanted to trust us. You *needed* to feel that trust and to give yourself over to someone . . .

ACTOR NO. 1 But in the end, it doesn't matter. Because we hold all the cards . . .

ACTRESS NO. 2 We are famous and you love us for that. Whatever we do or say or feel, you'll keep coming back. You'll watch our films and read magazines with our pictures on the cover and you'll wish you were us. Even marginally like one of us . . . but guess what? You won't be.

ACTRESS NO. 1 You just shelled out hard-earned cash for a ticket tonight. A ticket to see *us.* Now you'll try to get an autograph afterward or follow us out to the bar and think that, *magically*, you've become one of the in crowd . . . well, hey, grow up! Not gonna happen. Not tonight . . .

ACTOR NO. 2 . . . not ever. Uh-uh.

ACTRESS NO. 2 So go home. We've had our curtain call. We have your money.

ACTRESS NO. 1 And we don't like you. We don't wish to *befriend* you. I know that can be confusing because soon we'll be beaming into your homes and you'll see us on chat shows, always with these big smiles on our faces . . . but this is our *job.* To lie to you. We're liars. *Professional* liars. We lie and lie and lie again . . .

ACTOR NO. 1 Clap more if you'd like, but it won't help you now. We don't even really want your applause . . . in fact, here's some for you. For being our audience, and for being *so* easy . . .

ACTRESS NO. 2 . . . yeah. And so *fucking* stupid.

ACTRESS NO. 2 *begins to clap. Slowly at first but she builds in intensity. The others join her until they are all clapping furiously back at the audience.*

Silence. Darkness.

Neil LaBute

Union
Square

Production History

Union Square was first produced October 19, 2004, at the Michael Schimmel Center for the Arts at Pace University, New York. Director: John Rando. It was subsequently performed as part of the Downtown Plays at the first Tribeca Theater Festival.

MAN Josh Hamilton

Character

A MAN in his thirties

Setting

A thin patch of park in New York City

Silence. Darkness.

MAN *crosses toward us, carrying a crumpled fast-food bag under one arm. Smiles.*

MAN . . . excuse me? Yeah, hey, sorry. Hi. How ya doing? You good? Cool. That's great. I was, umm, can I ask you something, I mean, like, quick? Would that be all right? Thanks. (*Smiles.*) I'm . . . you probably couldn't tell or anything, but I'm new here, just visiting the city for a couple . . . whatever, it doesn't matter. I'm just, I came into that, what's it called, the Port Authority place there and I've been walking along, you know, heading downtown for a . . . I need to get myself downtown. I *am* headed south, right? I mean, this is, you can totally get yourself mixed up around here. Like, completely. I was, too, for about thirty minutes when I first got in, I asked somebody which way to go, but now that I think about it—it was this black kid, you know, with the jersey thing on and his hat all to one side—he was probably just messing with me. I bet that was it. Anyhow, he pointed like this and so I took off in that direction, but pretty soon I'm looking at the streets as I'm passing 'em and I'm like, "Hey, why're the numbers going *up* all the time?" Because I did look at a map before I got here, this lady on the bus had one of those fold-out jobbies in the little packet, they're pretty cool, and I had it out with her and we were studying the thing—her daughter had a baby and she's going to Queens or something like that to see her. Both of 'em. The mother *and* the baby, I'm saying.

Both. So we figured out the Queens thing and I checked out the whole layout of Manhattan, too, because that's where I'm headed, Manhattan. To *here*. (*Points*.) Sorry, got off the point there—I'll shut up soon, I promise! Anyway, this kid sends me uptown and the point I was trying to make before was that I should've known better because I already scouted it out on her thingie there. I noticed that the streets go up in numbers as you go north, I knew that, so it was just stupid of me to do what he said. That's what you get, though, by trusting a person you don't even know. And some black kid at that. Not that I'm prejudiced or whatnot, I'm not, I know lots of black guys, work with 'em all the time back home—I'm on a softball team, too, through the Parks & Rec department and we got a ton of black dudes in that league—so I'm not that way at all. I just mean he's a teenager, right, and teens can be kind of shitty that way, do things just to bug you or piss you off. Like that. Yeah. (*Beat*.) So there I am, walking and walking and walking and, suddenly, like some guy down at the power company flipped the breaker on in my head, I look up at one of those signs—maybe around Sixtieth Street or somewhere—and I say, I mean literally, like out loud, "Oh shit." Just like that. "Ohh shit." And I'm not a guy who swears all the time, not like my old man was, not at all, but it's warm out, you know—I mean feel it, it's sticky, right?—and I figure now I need to turn back around and walk downtown, so that stinks. It really does. See, I'm trying to not spend too much money or anything, conserve what I got, so I'm not gonna take any cab rides or that kind of deal, the subway or whatever, I was just planning on walking—I read this little booklet down at our public library before I left and New York was described as a "walking city." It was—so that's how I got back here. To where

Neil LaBute

I am now, here with you, Fourteenth Street or whatever. What
do they call this, Union Station or something? Square, Union
Square. Is that it? Yeah, Square. It's nice. Pretty. And hey,
look over there, a Starbucks! What a surprise . . . (*Laughs.*)
I'm kidding, that's probably an old joke here, but we've even
got one in our town now. I think there might even be *two*.
Maybe one down at the new mall they just put in. Haven't
been there yet but I heard there was one in the food court.
It's not, like, a regular mall or anything—you have to drive over
to Coeur d'Alene for that—but it's one of those outlet jobbies,
you know, with the big Ralph Lauren stores and Tommy Hilfiger
and that sort of stuff. Bargain shopping, you know what I'm
saying. Blah-blah-blah-blah! Sorry. God, I'm going on like a
schoolgirl here, I am sorry. Forgive me. Jesus. It's just . . . you
know, it's nice to actually talk to someone here, been walking
for a couple hours now and surrounded by people, I mean, an
ocean of people, everywhere you look, but not a word being
spoken. Not really. Just this constant hum, this sound all
around, cars and machines and horns and those sirens—
those things are, like, holy hell, that is like the loudest noise
I've ever heard!   but I haven't exchanged not two words of
conversation with anybody since I got here. And then I saw you
sitting there, just hunched up on your blanket, and I figured,
what the hell, he's not going anywhere fast, so I'll ask him.
That's what brought me over here, anyway. No offense. (*Beat.*)
So look, just point me toward, lemme see . . . (*Reaches in
pocket.*) I got a piece of this . . . an address here from my
wife . . . (*Reads.*) 221 Avenue A, number 3. See, that's what
was throwing me off before, I was walking around for a while
once I got down this far and I'm like, what the hell? Avenue A?
Kind of a name is that? I'm never gonna find it! That's why

I came over and asked, because that's the way I was raised. My mother was a sort of no-nonsense but very kind lady who just got shit done, you know? Got to it and got it done. She'd wash my mouth out with soap, probably, saying "shit" as much as I do—and she totally would, too, I promise you!—but other than that, she was a terrific person. It's not that bad, though, really, is it? Saying that? It just means . . . well, you know, "poop" or whatever, so who cares? I mean, really? We get so used to saying things, or hearing 'em, that they lose meaning, but a word like that, "shit" or some other ones that people think are curse words or swearing, they don't really bug me at all. Uh-uh, they don't. Not like they do my wife. Man, she hates that shit! (*Laughs.*) See? Sorry. It's just a habit . . . Anyhow, she gets so mad when I swear—she comes from a very, very strict family, Montana Methodists, which might be the tightest-assed people that God has ever created—and she gets all angry and crying and whatnot if I use any bad language at all. Even though she's, like, the black sheep of the family, that's what people would probably consider her, the wild one of the bunch . . . she still hates it when you swear! People are funny, aren't they? So complex and interesting, when you really think about it. Yep. (*Beat.*) She left me, my wife did—Cecily's her name, that's her given name, Cecily, which is kind of beautiful, I guess, but I always just called her CeeCee, which makes her smile—used to, anyway—and I like it. CeeCee. That doesn't really matter to you, though, I suppose, not to anybody who sleeps on a piece of *cardboard*, probably, but I just thought I'd give you a little background on us. Some, whatchamacallit . . . context? Yeah, that's it. Context. The context is, CeeCee took off on me—all that upbringing be damned—left me after six years of marriage and two kids at home. She moved away and wrote me a letter about three weeks ago, said she hated me—you believe that? Used that very word, "hate"—and says she's never coming back, don't bother looking for her or contacting her or nothing. She's done too much for people in her life and has bottled up her passions or some nonsense like that—women come up with some crazy stuff when they're angry or sad, don't they? I mean, "passions"! Please—and that she loves the children but she can't go on living a lie or something like that. I've got it here, with me, not that you'd care to read it, but I am carrying it with me. (*He produces it from a pocket, then puts it back.*) And you know what did it? Seriously, what set all this . . . shit . . . into motion? Huh? Jane Fonda. Not, like, the exercise tapes or anything like that, no, but a movie she saw on the TV. Yeah. Some older film that *Ms.* Fonda did a while back which I didn't even recognize—I was sitting right there, too, on the couch and half listening but I was tired and we'd just had dinner, some Boston Market so I was stuffed, and I notice that she's staring at the television, CeeCee is, and really into it. Leaning forward, like she does sometimes when *The View*'s on, or that Regis Philbin show. You know, *involved.* But it's getting late and I really wanna put ESPN on, check some of today's hockey highlights, but before I do, like the second before I click over on the remote, I glance at her and she gives me one of her looks. You know what I'm saying, one of those married looks that says "don't do it." If I want dinner tomorrow and clean socks and shit, do not touch that button. So I watch a little more—it was all snowy and I didn't even recognize any of the other actors—but eventually I give her a kiss on the head and wander off to bed. Figured what the hell, let her watch the damn thing . . . (*Checks his watch.*) Point being, she left me right after that. CeeCee did. Maybe only a month later, when I was at work one day. Kids're off at school. She packed it in and took off for here. New York City. (*Beat.*) Not that I ever would've known that, you know, where she went or anything, but that letter I mentioned, the one I just showed you, yeah . . . not only does it have the postmark on it but she writes her damn *address* up in the corner, like she was taught to do from the first day of kindergarten on! How about that one? Jesus, she makes me laugh sometimes, how, like, ordinary she is. For somebody who really thinks she's something special . . . (*Beat.*) That note was the first contact we've had, CeeCee and me, since she took off, like, six months ago. I mean, other than her lawyer . . . did I mention that before, all the lawyer business? That's a whole 'nother, believe me, you don't want me going off about that! Shit, it's . . . forget it. Basically, I'm paying for her little adventure, that's how that all worked out, I'm the money guy on her "I need to find myself" bullshit but I don't hear a word of this from the woman herself, oh no. I get some lawyer dude telling me all this, like he knows her so much better than me— "Cecily has requested," and, and, and, "Cecily will require," I mean, come on!—so you can imagine that when I get this letter from her, I'm more than a little surprised. Both surprised and delighted. And that's why I'm here . . . to see if we can, you know, whatever. Thought I'd drop in on her and see what we can figure out. CeeCee and me. (*He stops for a moment, glancing at a paper bag he's carrying.*) I see you got your eyes on my Burger King bag there, probably haven't heard a word I've said, right? Well, hate to break it to you, pal, but there's nothing in it, I mean, fries or anything like that. Half a Whaler or whatnot. Uh-uh. (*Whispers.*) Actually, I got a gun in here . . .

yeah, my old man's .357, a real beauty from the '60s. He left it to me when he died. Some kind of cancer took him a few years back and he left me this, this and one of his cars—my brother got the Corvette, which sucked—and a few hundred bucks. Sooooo . . . I got that letter, the one from CeeCee—telling me she's found a new *life* for herself, that she *escaped* and has now liberated herself from the slavery of marriage and some other Jane Fonda–inspired crap—I took a few days off from work, left the kids with my sister, and took the bus out here. Jumped on a Greyhound and made it in a couple days. And, well, hey, you know the rest. Except for my run-in with that black kid, I've been enjoying myself just fine. Seeing the sights, taking my time. Just walking. And in a minute or two, once I get my bearings down here . . . (*He looks around.*) . . . it's like being in the Grand Canyon or something, how I'd imagine it, at least—never been—and trying to get back up to the rim by suppertime. Or maybe not, shit, I'm just rambling now, so forget it. But . . . I will find that address, I will, this A Street or wherever she's living now, ol' CeeCee, and I'm gonna go and knock on her door, *knock-knock*, and when she opens it, I'm gonna walk up to her and put the barrel of this revolver right down her throat. I am. I'm gonna do that and then I'll smile at her, yeah, smile down at her and lean in real close, all up in her face and whisper, "Was it worth it, CeeCee? Finding yourself like that?" because I'm curious, I am, I really wanna know if it was . . . right before I blow her fucking head off. (*Smiles.*) Then I'm off to the terminal, I got a nine-fifteen leaving here tonight and back to work on Monday. Oh yeah, I need to mess up her place a little bit, too, make sure it looks like some local punks broke in there. See, I got it all worked out . . . the whole business. Came up with that ransacking-the-place thing in Ohio or somewhere! It's a good idea, right? (*A beat, then a big smile. A laugh.*) I'm just yanking your chain, buddy, seriously! Damn! I thought you New Yorkers were so quick and clever or whatever. Jesus. Look at you, with your mouth all hanging open there! I'm *kidding*!! I don't give a shit what CeeCee does, we're better off without her. Just thought I'd drop in on her on my vacation, say hello. Figure out some legal stuff. Hey, don't worry about it . . . (*He checks his watch.*) So I'm outta here, need to get on the road, all right? Nice chatting with you. And which way am I going again? To Avenue A? (*Motions.*) That way? Okay . . . I'm trusting you now, don't pull that ghetto shit on me! I'm just playing around. It's cool . . . (*He reaches into his bag.*) Here . . . oh, no, wait, can't give you that! (*Another laugh.*) Kidding! (*Reaches into his pocket and produces a few bucks.*) There, knock yourself out, have a feast on me. I'll see you around . . . (*He starts off.*) What's that shit people always say to each other, you know, like in the movies all the time, although you never hear it in life? You know, ummmm . . . oh yeah. I got it. Hey, man . . . have a nice day.

The MAN *smiles again and waves, walking off into the passing crowd.*

Silence. Darkness.

Neil LaBute

Love at Twenty

Production History

Love at Twenty was produced December 5, 2005, at Circle in the Square, New York, as part of the "Twenty" Benefit by MCC for their twentieth anniversary celebration. Director: John Rando.

YOUNG WOMAN Lauren Ambrose

Character

A YOUNG WOMAN just turning twenty

Setting

A college campus, probably in the Midwest

Silence. Darkness.

Lights up on a YOUNG WOMAN *standing onstage, looking down at us. A cell phone in one hand. Purse over the other shoulder.*

YOUNG WOMAN . . . 1-2-3-4-5-6-7-8-9-10-11-12-13-14-15-16-17-18-19—and 20! Ready or not, here I come. (*Smiles.*) God, do you remember that from when we were kids and you'd play games, like hide-and-seek or crap like that, and one person would be "it," covering their eyes and counting to twenty or however many and then you'd have to go find everybody or run around, that kind of thing? Yeah . . . that was fun. Really, really fun stuff. I loved doing all that, and being "it," too, I never minded that. Uh-uh, I didn't at all, which a lot of kids never wanted to do—especially most of the girls I grew up around—because they'd get scared or stupid shit like that, being alone in the dark or whatever, but not me. Nope, I didn't mind it one bit, being that person . . . I guess I sort of like being the center of attention. A *lot.*

She laughs and stops a moment, checking her phone.

YOUNG WOMAN And I never, I mean, at that age I had no idea how important that number would end up being to me. In my life. Twenty. It really, really is because I'm, like, practically that age now. Going to be, anyway, in a few weeks—December, that's my birthday. Not the whole month, obviously, but during it. *On* the twentieth, which absolutely sucks because it's so close to the holidays that I always get screwed on gifts—"We'll just do it all together, on Christmas, and you'll get extra." My folks tried to sell me on that one when I was little . . . that I was so extra-special that we should just pretend that me and baby Jesus had the same birthday, but all it meant was, like, maybe one or two more gifts than my sister got and not even anything big, 'cause my Easy-Bake Oven (for instance) was the major package and my mom and dad'd just toss in a few other little bits—clothes, even!—and that'd be that. That was my birthday, which stinks. Completely. So, yeah, that's me . . . almost twenty. On the twentieth. And what else? I mean, since I said it was such a huge deal . . . oh, yeah, right. This guy I'm seeing, well, he's my professor, actually, in this one history course—it's my second year at college, so that's cool—he's almost exactly twenty years older than me. Yep. "Twenty years your senior," my mom says, which is so gay because she's only, like, twenty-*three* years older than me but she sounds like my grandma or something . . . she always says shit like that, but especially about him. My boyfriend. Well, I guess he's not actually that, technically, because he's got a wife and all that—no kids, though—and that's a bit of a bummer but he's getting divorced, he totally is, but they've just got a few things to work out. Legalities and all that crap and I've been very good about waiting for him. We started in together last semester—I'm only taking his "Empire Building from Napoleon to Nixon" because it fits my schedule and it's first thing in the morning so he can give me a ride (my Honda is a piece of shit when it's cold)—but yeah, we've been a couple for almost a year now, school year, anyway, and he's promised me that we're always gonna be together. Forever. (*Beat.*) Well, until today, that is. Like twenty minutes ago . . .

Neil LaBute

She stops and checks her phone again, then her watch.

YOUNG WOMAN Sorry . . . I'm waiting for a call. See, he just texted
me. Dexter did. That's him—Dex, I call him—and he sent me
this juicy message about how good it was last night and how
much he adores being in my mouth and, you know, all that
stuff . . . but actually, I was at Tula's last night, this bar
downtown where I work—okay, dance—and I haven't seen him
since Tuesday so, umm, that's weird. But the hurtful part of it
is, the actual *bad* part of it is this: It's to his wife. Kimmie.
That's her name—which really makes me want to barf
whenever I hear him say it—not some other student or lady in
town, which I could then understand because he's quite good-
looking and sexy and all that for this older guy, but it's meant
for his *wife* who he is supposed to be leaving and so that
means he's lying to me, right? Lying and sleeping with her and
all that shit that he's been telling me, assuring me is just not
true. And now I know for, like, a fact . . . is. Yeah. Dexter's
actually screwing me *and* Kimmie and God knows who else
and you know what? That just really doesn't work for me . . .
(*Beat.*) Dex seems to be doing a little "empire building" of his
own and I figure that shit has just gotta stop. Right? So—
I sent a little message of my own, a few minutes ago, to his
wife, Kimmie (seriously, can you believe that name?!). One
sentence, twenty little words that very succinctly—an adverb
I learned from the big man himself—explain our present
situation, and how he tastes in *my* mouth, you know, that sort
of deal. On their home phone. Then, and here's the kicker
part . . . I texted Dex and told him what's up. Sent it to him on
his way to some faculty meeting and told him what I've done,
said that he's got a few minutes to make his choice—skip out

Love at Twenty

and run home to erase the thing before "the wife" can get back (Kimmie works for a dentist—gross!) or stand up and take it like a man, do all the shit he's been promising me for so many months now . . . it's entirely up to him. *Or* it could come down to, you know, like, fate or whatever, if he doesn't get my message and Kimmie wanders on back after going to the grocery store—she's supposed to be like this major cook or something—and then she'll hear it all and confront him or call me and if she does, if *that* is the case, then I'll fill her in on what's what. I definitely will if that's what happens, I've already promised myself. (*Beat.*) So you can imagine all my anticipation . . . right? I mean, your whole life can change, just like that, in twenty minutes . . . Bam! (*Snaps her fingers.*) Kooky, isn't it?

She looks down at her phone again. Clicks it open, checks it.

YOUNG WOMAN I mean, what would you do? Right? Sometimes you've really just got to get in there and get your hands dirty when you believe in something so intensely, and this is one of those times . . . Dex and I are gonna be so happy, so stupendously fucking happy when all this stuff of his gets straightened out. I really believe that. Or not. Or he will scurry home like some total pussy and fix things for a minute and then I'll know he's not the man I want or need him to be and at the tender age of twenty I'm gonna realize that it's a long road ahead to happiness. But, hey, at least I'll know, right? At least I'll head off into the sunset with my eyes wide open and understand a bit more about the way this world works . . . and that's something, isn't it? Yeah. At least I'll have that . . .

Neil LaBute

Suddenly her phone rings. She looks out at us one last time.

YOUNG WOMAN Oh, wow. Here we go . . . 1-2-3-4-5-6-7-8-9-10-11-12-13-14-15-16-17-18-19—and 20! (*Smiles.*) Ready or not, here I come . . .

She lets it ring twice more, then goes to answer it.

YOUNG WOMAN . . . hello?

Silence. Darkness.

Land of
the Dead

Production History

Land of the Dead was first produced on September 9, 2002, at Town Hall in New York City as part of the Brave New World Festival. Director: Neil LaBute.

MAN Paul Rudd

WOMAN Kristin Davis

Characters

Setting

New York City—on the day

Silence. Darkness.

Lights up slowly on a MAN *and a* WOMAN, *seated apart.*

MAN   Wow. What a day . . . I mean, *what* a day, right?

WOMAN   I'll never forget it . . .

MAN   You know, because, it's not . . . that kinda thing doesn't just come around any ol' time of the week, thank God. Huh? That's one of those dates that gets in your head and stays there. Like, ahh . . . ahh . . .

WOMAN   I got up around three that morning, I remember that. Very clearly. Must've been around, umm . . . well, no later than three-fifteen, anyway. Right about then. It was before dawn, I know that. It was dark out our window and I just couldn't sleep, what with it still being warm outside, even so early, it was warm and I was uncomfortable and so I got up. Maybe three-thirty but no later than that . . . (*Beat.*) He was still snoring . . .

MAN   I was out cold. That night? I mean, completely zonked. I'd been out with some of the guys I work with, my buddies, and so by the time I got home I was staggering, not ashamed to admit it. We'd closed a big deal that afternoon and you gotta take a minute, pound the ol' fists on the chest a bit when something good happens, right? I always do. Anyway, I slept great . . .

WOMAN   I go to my purse and begin to count the money again. That's stupid to do, I know, I know that, I must've checked the thing, like, *sixty* times already, but what else am I gonna do?

Land of the Dead

It's three-thirty in the morning, or four. Something like that. Whatever. I count it out again. Should be four hundred dollars. In tens . . .

MAN She made me go out to an ATM that night! I'm sloshing around like that drunk guy off *The Andy Griffith Show*—the hell was his name again? Oscar, or Otis, something like that, Otis, I think—and I'm tired, I gotta work in the morning. She's sitting up when I get in, just after midnight, and she's sitting on the love seat and just staring at me . . . says I shouldn't have taken any money from there without telling her— I snagged a few bills out for the bar—and I need to go back out. So I empty my wallet, dig through the sock drawer, anyplace I might've jammed a spare twenty, but it's no good. We're fifty bucks short. Great. I'm looking at her face and she's not saying anything and I know not to argue. I just slip my jacket back on and head down to the corner. There's a Citibank, like, three blocks over . . .

WOMAN I was waiting for him to get that money—I didn't care about his being out that night, partying, that was fine. Not like it was some big surprise—I just wanted the rest of the cash. I suppose now, when I think about it, we could've just written a check, but I didn't . . . I wanted to pay it, bill by bill, putting it out there on the counter, so I'd remember. So I'd feel it. Feel something.

MAN Normally I would go with her, no question. Seriously. We'd talked about it and I promised I would and so, yeah, under *normal* circumstances I totally would've been there. Absolutely yes . . . but the boss is all over me this morning, wants to go to breakfast, he's calling my cell by six o'clock, busting out of his pants he's so happy with our closing that account that he's not taking no for an answer . . . I *have* to go. I mean, if you knew the guy, he's just . . . anyhow, she understands. Once I explain it, she completely understands . . .

WOMAN Typical, right? He leaves it up to me . . . but what're you gonna do? Get into this, like, big *thing* over coffee about something that is just not gonna change? I guess you could, some women might, but that's not me. It's not, and I don't feel the need to make up excuses. He'd just sit there, anyway, reading *People* magazine and checking his watch, so forget it . . . at that point we'd decided, we're doing it, might as well just get it done.

MAN She leaves a little bit before me . . . maybe ten minutes ahead. This peck on the cheek and she takes off. Leaves the stupid money on the table! So I'm running downstairs in my bare feet to catch her . . . believe that?

WOMAN He comes barreling down the stairs, yelling out my name and chasing me. For a second, I mean, just a *moment* there . . . I thought he wanted to talk, change of heart or something like that. I can recall turning around, standing over by the mailboxes there, this huge smile on my face . . . then I see the envelope in his hand. He's sort of out of breath . . .

MAN I hand her the thing and then, you know, like on *impulse*, I kiss her again because it's, I mean, it feels like the thing to do . . . and then I go up and have a shower. Watch a little ESPN before heading out to Applebee's . . .

WOMAN I took the earliest appointment I could . . . seven-thirty. I thought that was the best thing, you know, just get it over with. Take a little time, but I'm still back to work by lunch. Only have to use up half a personal day that way. (*Beat.*) The thirty-fourth floor. Sitting in the waiting room of this squat gray building, I practically have the whole place to myself. A young girl—a teenager, I'm sure—a few chairs down. I look around for a magazine to read, something, but no issues of *People* anywhere. That makes me laugh . . .

MAN Breakfast is pretty decent. I have ham on the bone, and some sorta eggs. White toast, which is not the most healthy thing in the world, I know, I know, but hey . . . a hangover the size of *Delaware* up there above my eyes. The boss is droning on and on about production and output and I'm just staring at him, wishing he'd been hit by a taxi as he was crossing the street on the way over, so I could enjoy my food in peace . . . that's a lousy thing to say, but it's how I'm feeling.

WOMAN They call my name fifteen minutes later . . .

MAN This is around seven forty-five or so. I check my watch right about then . . .

WOMAN I'd already done the forms and everything, so I go right in. Into one of their rooms there . . .

MAN Food's good but the guy is driving me nuts, talking loud and this little bit of jelly hanging on his bottom lip as he's yakking away. I mean, hell, I might as well have gone with her to the clinic, the way he's carrying on . . . least I could've read a *magazine* or something.

WOMAN I'm perched on the edge of the table there, up on the table with that kind of crinkly paper under me . . . and the nurse is saying something. I remember quite clearly: She said, "I love your hair." Then, "I hate your earrings," which kind of catches me off guard, and later, "There'll be some slight discomfort." (*Beat.*) I still have the earrings . . .

MAN No, I'm pro-choice, I am . . . she can choose to keep the kid, or she can choose to keep me. It's entirely up to her! (*Laughs.*) That's a joke, actually, I heard that at work . . . kinda funny. Yep. (*Beat.*) But seriously, think about it . . . what's the problem? You do it, it happens, it's over. It really is that simple. Anyway, I've heard that it doesn't hurt that much—and I mean in terms of physical pain—at least no more than a pretty good paper cut. Now, I know, I know, there's a whole "psychological" thing going on, I know that. But come on . . . we're still talking about, in essence, a *paper cut*! I mean, who hasn't had one of those? (*Beat.*) Hell, I'd do the thing *myself* if I had the right attachment for the DustBuster, so I'm probably the wrong person to be asking . . .

WOMAN And I don't really feel anything afterward. Nothing . . . They say I can stay there as long as I need, which is nice, I thought. I sleep for a while—I didn't have to, I really don't feel anything at all, that's the truth, but—I do sleep. A little. (*Beat.*) Someone comes in a bit later to check on me, so I get my things together and go up to the front to pay. At the last moment—I mean, I even reached out and snatched back the envelope—I decide to pay by credit card instead, which somehow seems, I don't know, appropriate. I put it on my Diners Club. (*Laughs.*) I'm not kidding, they actually take my card!

MAN Besides, we're sending it to a better place, right? Better than this world, anyways . . . Or maybe not. Maybe it is wrong, hell, I don't know, but you gotta believe something, you do, otherwise . . . Not that I wouldn't've taken care of it. No, seriously! I can see myself buying toys, changing diapers, stuff like that . . . easily. It would've been nice. Forming that parental bond, going to school plays, I could've done that. Yeah, I would enjoy a child. I know I would . . . (*Beat.*) Of course, all that's easier to say knowing that the little bundle's safely in some incinerator somewhere. Know what I mean? Oh, come on . . . sure you do. (*Beat.*) Anyway, I leave her a message on my way to the office . . .

WOMAN I stop on the street there and listen to him, tuck myself into a doorway and listen. I can tell he's just finished his meal because he's kind of sucking at his teeth, not all the time, but every once in a while . . . this kind of sucking sound while it's being recorded. And as he speaks, he just casually tosses this in: "I tried phoning you earlier, but I couldn't get through . . ."

MAN I tried a couple times before I ate, I really did . . . but she's always switching the power thing off on the side there. Drives me nuts!

WOMAN He says, "'Cause I was gonna say, I mean, if you wanna, we can go ahead and just keep the thing. Up to you." (*Beat*.) I stand there for a minute, supporting myself against the metal doorjamb and not able to speak. My mouth opening and closing for a second, and then I say out loud, not *to* anyone but say it aloud . . . "Too late . . . it's too *late*. I already did it . . ." I have to play it back a few times . . . just to take it all in . . .

MAN The whole morning just sucks, I mean, you know . . . what with the way she's acting about the phone afterward—it's like, come on, just *take* the call!—plus I'm running late . . . it's turning out to be a bad, bad day! Wish I hadn't even got up, honestly, that's exactly how I'm feeling by the time I snag a taxi. Wish I was still lying in bed . . .

WOMAN And I'm okay, it's . . . it's no problem. The only . . . I shouldn't even bring this up, but . . . (*Beat*.) I keep hearing that sound. That buzzing, you know, from the . . . I'm still aware of it. (*Listens*.) There . . . can you hear that? Right there. Listen. Can you? It's . . .

MAN Anyhow, I get upstairs, over to my cubicle, and just kick back for a second. Take a breath. Look out at the city.

Neil LaBute

WOMAN It's beautiful as I'm heading home . . . outside, I mean.
I decide to walk back instead of taking a cab. Stupid, but I
want to . . . I just need to be lost for a while, on the
streets . . .

MAN And you know, I don't care what's going on in your life—
money troubles, difficulties with your lady, whatever—a view
like this just perks you up. It really does.

WOMAN Sometimes, as you're moving along, it sounds like a
thousand twangling instruments humming in your ears . . .
and you can let yourself be swallowed up.

MAN Up here, in these cloud-capped towers, all your worries and
fears and just, you know, bad *stuff* . . . melts into air, into thin
air. The sky's clear as anything. All blue. Makes you feel, I
dunno . . . alive, I guess . . .

For a moment, the earsplitting sound of jet aircraft. Deafening.

The light over the MAN *slowly goes out. The* WOMAN *removes a cell
phone from her purse.*

WOMAN I kept trying his phone after they said . . . ringing it, just
ringing it and hoping that he'd pick up, answer it or something,
all night long. For a few days, actually . . . but he didn't. He
never did . . . (*Beat.*) I still have that message he left me, the
one about not going through with it, about keeping the . . .
I have to save it every week or so, listen again and save it
or it'll disappear. It'll just . . . be gone. So I play it at night
sometimes, when I'm lying there, missing him. Both of them.
I'll play the thing . . .

She presses a button and holds the phone to her ear.

Land of the Dead

MAN (*in darkness*) "Hey, it's me . . . breakfast was okay, not bad. Anyway, I tried you earlier, but, listen . . . I was gonna say, I mean, if you wanna, we can go ahead and just keep the thing. Up to you. Or whatever . . . let's just speak later. Call me if you need to. I was gonna go pick up the Hawaii pictures from the photo place, I went by, but they don't open until nine and I wanna be in a bit early, get a little paperwork done . . . 'kay. Buzz me later. Love ya."

WOMAN It's funny, the stuff you remember . . . Well, not *funny*, but, you know. Yeah . . . (*Listens.*) There . . . there's that buzzing again. It's right . . . is that my phone, or . . . ? Do you hear that? Do you? Listen . . .

She checks her cell phone again, then looks around, searching.

Silence. Darkness.

Neil LaBute

Stand-Up

Production History

Stand-Up was first performed on January 31, 2005, for an MCC benefit at Circle in the Square Theater—the evening was titled "Escape: Six Ways to Get Away." Director: Erica Gould.

MAN Mos Def

Character

MAN—in his early thirties

Setting

An empty stage

Silence. Darkness.

MAN *walks out into a spotlight, stands next to a microphone.*
Squints. Looks around, tries to smile. Nearly pulls it off.

MAN . . . I've got ten minutes. (*Beat.*) I mean, not to live or
anything, I don't mean to make it sound so serious—I'm not
desperate, got *leukemia* or whatever—I'm just saying, ten
minutes is what they gave me. Out here, in front of you.
People. I get ten minutes to be up here and try out all my . . .
well, you know. Whatchamacallit. My act. Or, or, or, my . . .
material. I guess that's what they say, like, professionals do.
They call it that. Their "material." So somebody keep an eye
on their watch, okay, don't let me run over. Ten minutes and
then I'm outta here. Promise. (*Smiles.*) I mean, gimme a little
breathing room, like, if I'm in the middle of a joke or whatnot,
lemme, you know, finish that . . . but otherwise, finger across
the throat and I'll get the message. (*Demonstrates.*) It's my
first time, so I'm gonna just go for it here, see what I got. Be
honest with me—gentle but honest—if my stuff stinks I should
know that, so lemme know. I mean, keep all the flying beer
bottles and shit to a minimum, if you can, but if you boo, then
you boo. That's the exciting thing about this performing deal,
right? The immediacy of it all. This moment between me and
all of, ahh . . . I actually can't tell if there's anybody out there,
that light's in my face, so . . . a little laughter might help.
(*Waits.*) With an emphasis on "little." Okay, I get it . . . I need
to earn my keep. Fair enough. All right, let's see . . . maybe a

quick bit of background on me would help, that's probably a good place to, ummmmm . . . yeah. My name's Merrit, Merrit Wilson, I think the guy introducing everybody said it, but just in case you were in the john or rifling through your girlfriend's purse while she was . . . I'm Merrit Wilson. Hello. Or, good evening. That's what most guys say who do this for a living— which I don't yet, obviously—Good evening, everyone. Hey. Welcome. I'm Merrit Wilson. (*Beat.*) Wow, I suck so far, right? I mean . . . just sort of stepping away from myself, I mean, like, hovering above us right now, if I were to do that and I'm looking down on this . . . I really do suck. And, see, I told folks I would, that I'd be lousy at this—I work with a bunch of people at this computer company; I don't wanna blurt out the name because then it would seem like I'm plugging the place and I'm really not, honestly, but I work there—started about six months ago when I first moved here; I'm from Chicago, well, outside Chicago, actually, Glen Ellyn—and I'm, you know how it is when you're the new person at a place, work, or the gym or that kind of thing . . . you wanna make an impression, be responded to as an individual, so I've got all this nervous energy, sitting in a chair all day, and it needs to get out somehow, so I start telling jokes. Not like "knock-knock" farmer's-daughter stuff, not at all, or political junk—"My grandmother died at Auschwitz and all I got was this lousy T-shirt"—no, but just little observations about people, or mimicking our boss, an impression or two, that type of deal. And so, pretty soon . . . I'm the, you know, in-house funny guy. The equivalent of the class clown or whatever. And that's all cool because, hey, it's nice to be loved and so, ahh, blah-blah-blah . . . one day at lunch, we're over at this sushi place just off Houston—it's very good, the name is . . . well, one of

Neil LaBute

those Japanese ones, which always sounds like my dad taking a shit when I try and say it . . . (*Makes several grunting sounds.*) . . . but it's terrific and you should try it. All of you, right after this. *I'm* buying. Seriously, meet me there and I'll . . . (*Looks out.*) How'm I doing on time? (*Waits.*) Silence. Silence. It's like a Bergman movie out there. (*Laughs.*) I don't even know what that means . . . I think I heard Woody Allen say something like that in a movie once, or on one of his records, which are hilarious, by the way. Now that is some funny shit, Woody Allen recordings, you should be so lucky that he was here and doing some of that . . . the moose thing, remember? Killer. But you're not . . . lucky, I'm saying. No. You're not, you're not lucky, you're stuck with me, so just sit back and shut up. I'm working on it, I'm building up here, getting ready for the jokes . . . promise. Any time now and they're gonna just come pouring out of me, because I'm a funny guy and I can do this. (*Beat.*) All right, so there's these two guys . . . no, wait, that already stinks. I can tell. Any joke that starts like that is gonna be crap, like your *uncle* telling it, so forget it. I'm starting over. All right. Here we go . . . (*Smiles.*) Hi, I'm Merrit Wilson, good evening. Anybody from out of town? Anyone? A few people, cool, that's . . . no, come on, what's that? Jesus, no. Uh-uh. "Out of town"?! That is just so lame . . . (*Beat.*) See, I've seen so many people do this, on the *Tonight Show* or whatever, *Letterman*, that I've got all the opening bits down, the walking out here, the banter and stuff, but—I'll be honest with you—my jokes suck. They just, like, absolutely reek. They're not even jokes, really, I mean, not actually, they just, you know . . . I can observe things. In the moment. React. Throw a little irony out there and get a smile out of my coworkers. That's what I do. Not this. I'm wasting

Stand-Up

your time here, so I'm gonna . . . sorry. (*Starts off.*) No. I'm not gonna do that, no. Walk off. I'm—I've gone through this, done this routine in the mirror about a *million* times and I'm ready, so . . . it's open mike night, right? I mean, you guys come here expecting this kind of thing, at least sorta, and I'm . . . no. I will do this. A lot of my colleagues are out there . . . (*Looks around.*) . . . supposed to be, anyhow—I'm gonna be at the door later and check your names off a list, I promise!— so, here I go. Do or die. (*Long beat.*) Okay . . . I'm gonna come clean here, quickly, I mean, because I know I'm running low on . . . I don't give a shit about the comedy part. Being a comic, not really. Not that you could tell or anything! (*Laughs.*) I thought this would just be a really great opportunity, like, a huge AA meeting or something—I'm not a drinker, but I'm just saying—to stand up in front of people, some people I know even, one girl in particular . . . I hope you're out there, initials are J.S. . . . because I need to let you guys know that I'm, well . . . you know. Not who I say I am. Or appear to be, or . . . like that. All my life I've been this guy who had to—this isn't a sob story or anything, it's really not, but—my folks are older and the kind of town that I grew up in . . . all I'm saying is I moved here, came to New York to just be me, to see if I could, you know . . . escape, sort of. Be free. And I took this job and I wanted to fit in and so, yeah, I start with the funny crap and you guys—I hope some of them are here or this is really embarrassing!—you accepted me and I even got into a little bit of a relationship, dating or whatever, and I'm . . . (*Beat.*) I just really can't go on doing this, being that person for you now, because that's not why I came here. Picked up and left a good job with benefits and came to Manhattan with all my savings because I need to be me. Okay? I have to be . . .

Neil LaBute

(*getting flustered*) I'm gay. All right? I am a fag, or whatever you're gonna say behind my back about me. There—I like men and I like sex with men and I do not wanna be ashamed of that anymore. I don't. I'm—my first day I came to work, all excited about being here and found this great apartment and I'm, like, not even in the door, I was in the *elevator* . . . and two guys, I'm not naming names, but . . . two guys from my department are snickering about this delivery boy. He gets off on seven and some snide comment about his biking shorts and all this . . . it doesn't matter. You know what you said. And looking over at me to see how I take it . . . and my, you know, my heart just crashes, it does, drops to the floor right there and I'm thinking, "Well, shit, here we go. Here we go *again*." And I'm figuring, hell, I might as well be back home with my father and brother and listening to their bullshit about how God feels about homos and AIDS is a righteous disease and, fuck . . . so I thought I'd come here tonight and stand up . . . you know, just stand up one time in my life and be a man. I mean, like, a real man and be truthful and open and if you can accept that, accept all that about me . . . well, then, I only took up ten minutes of your time but you'll have given *me* a lifetime of blessings. (*Smiles.*) So, thanks a lot . . .

Applause. He waits, then bursts out laughing. Suddenly the MAN *has a much stronger stage presence.*

MAN Hey, hey, come on, what're you people, *gay*?! Jesus . . . I'm kidding! It's a joke, some new material I'm working on. Anybody remember Andy Kaufman, for God's sake?!! Jeez, what a bunch of morons. I've lived here all my life, from Flushing, and I love girls, I'm totally straight. In fact, I hate fags—no offense, guys, I'm sure it's a beautiful thing, I just hate any sex that ends with me wiping shit off my dick—but I love all you people, you've been great, I mean it. And damn easy! Jesus, I could actually hear a few chicks sniffling out there . . . (*Grins.*) My name's not Merrit, by the way; if it was I'd kill myself—well, my *parents* first, then me—it's Danny Patrick, and I'm at Geno's Laugh Riot on Thursdays, it's over on Twelfth, and I'll be at the Comic Strip starting on Saturday evening. That's *Saturday* evening, so get out your styluses and add it to your fucking Palm Pilots, you yuppie pricks, and we'll see you there—unless you're gay—just kidding! All you cocksuckers can come, too, if you want. Just not on me! (*Laughs.*) I'm joking! Sort of . . . Good night, everybody!!

MAN *waves and moves briskly offstage. Pool of light remains.*

Silence. Darkness.

Neil LaBute

Coax

Production History

Coax was performed on March 7, 2002, at Primary Stages in New York City. Director: Tyler Merchant.

YOUNG MAN Michael Friedman

YOUNG WOMAN Andrea Anders

NOTE: This play has subsequently also been performed under the title *I Really, Really Like You.*

Characters

YOUNG MAN—in his mid-twenties
YOUNG WOMAN—almost thirty

Setting

An empty stage or a quiet coffee shop (you be the judge)

NOTE: A slash in dialogue denotes a suggested point of overlap between that line and the next actor's line.

Silence. Darkness.

YOUNG MAN *standing at a sandwich bar, pacing a bit near a round standing table. Bottle of spring water in one hand. He notices us. He carries a manuscript.*

YOUNG MAN Hey! Hello there, how's it going . . . are you . . . ? . . . no. Sorry. I didn't, I'm looking for . . . doesn't matter. Thanks anyway . . .

He takes a gulp from the bottle. Looks back at us, smiles.

YOUNG MAN I don't know why I even said that, "are you . . . ?" because, I mean, look, you're obviously not the person I'm waiting for. (*Points to script.*) Says so right here. I realize that, I must've . . . you know, it's just that whole weird "theater" thing, right? I mean, you can see me, I know you're there, but hey, let's just pretend it's "real," let's all sit here and act like I'm this college guy who's hanging out in some local spot, waiting to meet up with someone . . . but none of it's really happening, is it? I mean, that's what we're taught to believe, anyway. That's the idea. I could never get my head around that stuff, I mean, that kinda concept. The "fourth wall" thing. It's just so . . . odd. See, I took some theater in college, I mean "drama," that's what they liked to call it where I went to school, "draaa-ma." Big deal, right? Same difference. Anyhow, I took an intro course once, and this sort of little acting thing, improv or whatever, and I was okay, not like some Charlie Chaplin or anything but kinda good. I had no problem getting up in front of people, or pretending to be somebody else. That was easy. But I could never totally get into that whole "suspension of disbelief" thing. I mean, what the hell does that mean? Why am I watching this crap if I'm full of disbelief? Right? I should be down in the lobby getting my money back, or free passes or something! It just doesn't sound right, "disbelief." And then, nobody could ever set me straight, either, like, fully explain it. I'd say to my teacher, I'd say to the guy, "Well, wouldn't it at least be suspension of *belief*?" because that's what you're really doing—saying okay, fine, whatever, you're a sailor or an ostrich or, or, or who knows what. Hamlet, maybe. But they're not, right, they never really are, they're some *sophomore* in tights, but I'm saying, "Yeah, okay, just for tonight, for the next couple hours . . . I'll believe you, whatever you tell me." And he'd say, my professor would, he'd go, "Yes, right, that's the idea, but it's disbelief that you're putting on hold, not belief. It's the other way 'round." He'd always do that, right in front of the whole class, with this sort of big, affected accent thing. "It's the other way *'round*." Okay, man, whatever. (*Beat.*) Anyway, I got a C in there. Which kinda sucked . . .

He takes another drink.

YOUNG MAN I mean, think about it, though, the whole thing's confusing. I'm here, I am, I'm right up here, standing in front of you. That's really happening, isn't it? It's true. So does that make me an actor, or just some guy who's waiting to see somebody, this girl that I met? I dunno, you decide. I mean,

Neil LaBute

I'm not famous, right, not some *thespian*—that's another word they taught us, which is so gay. True? "Thespian." I don't mean like gay-gay, like homo-gay or just because it sounds like, well, you know, women in "love," but it's just so . . . I'm not sure, something. Self-important, I guess. Anyway, it used to make us laugh—but I'm not like that, some well-known person who you see on the TV all the time but harboring, like, this secret passion to go perform a play somewhere. The Neighborhood Playhouse or whatnot. I'm not! You don't know me, I could be anybody. I'm just some dude waiting to see this girl that I hooked up with. At least that's how I figure it. But you . . . you guys are sitting there, thinking, "Shut up," maybe, or, "This guy talks too much . . ." And you're also pretty sure I'm an actor, doing my stuff, and this is all made up and part of the thing. This whole evening you're watching. But me, that's not how I picture it at all. I am here, the girl's coming, and we're gonna have a great night. So see how blurry all that reality/illusion crap can get, I mean, when you really think about it? Wow . . .

He checks his watch.

YOUNG MAN She's late . . . or is it just not her cue yet? (*Smiles.*) Anyway, as I was saying . . . look, right here. I was thirsty so I bought some water, see? (*Holds up the bottle.*) And that's totally water inside of there. It is! (*Takes a drink.*) Umm . . . nice. Bet you wish you had some. So look, here I am, I'm here, I'm waiting, I got my drink, so what's the truth? Actor, some guy? Hey, whatever. You figure it out . . .

He glances off, spots someone.

Coax

YOUNG MAN I think this might be her . . . hold on. (*He gestures offstage.*) Hey! Hello . . . how's it going? (*back to us*) This looks like her, I mean, from her description of herself. I think she's grabbing a coffee or something. A latte or who knows what . . . be over in a second. So . . . I'm really looking forward to this, she sounds great. Really cute. See, we met online, not like in a chat room or anything, I don't really get into all that, sitting and talking about music or whatever, but I'll hang around just outside one, you know, like where you can read the names of who's in there, and then I'll just randomly e-mail 'em or strike up one of those instant message things and that'll usually do it . . . I mean, sometimes. A lot of them, girls, I mean, are totally short with you on there, cut you off if you ask anything private or get at all sexy with 'em, but sometimes they're pretty great about it. Really trusting. And I so dig that . . . you know, that moment when one crosses over. The line, I mean, just gets up and trots over the line right to where you are. That is perfect. That is . . . complete spiritual joy to me . . . that moment, I mean, just before, when you don't know if it's gonna happen or not. And then it does. And then she's yours . . .

A YOUNG WOMAN *enters, holding a cup of coffee. She smiles lightly, puts her hand out to the* YOUNG MAN, *who warmly takes it in his.*

YOUNG WOMAN . . . hello?

YOUNG MAN Hi . . . are you?

YOUNG WOMAN Shelly. Yeah, I am./Hi. I'm late, but your directions were kinda . . . this is *way* out here!

YOUNG MAN Hey there!/I know, sorry, but it's great to meet you. *Finally* . . .

YOUNG WOMAN I know, right?/It's crazy . . .

YOUNG MAN After, like, four months!/Exactly. Didn't think it'd
happen . . .

YOUNG WOMAN I know, I know . . . and we're, like, what, *six* miles
away from each other? Something like that . . .

YOUNG MAN Yeah. Well, maybe ten . . . the school's over in . . .

YOUNG WOMAN Oh, right, right, you're still on campus you said, so
that's . . . (*Spills her coffee.*) Oww, shit!/Aaahh . . .

YOUNG MAN You all right?!/Here, let me . . .

YOUNG WOMAN No, it's okay, I just . . . lemme grab some
napkins . . .

She wanders off, licking the side of her paper cup.

YOUNG MAN Seems nice . . . (*back to us*) She's cute, huh? Yeah.
Really cute. And they're not all that way, believe me. Ones I've
met. People are usually sorta misleading when you talk to 'em
on your laptop . . . Smarter. Better looking. Or richer. The
whole thing . . . you can easily be whatever you wanna be
when you're floating around out there in cyberspace. It's a
dopey name, cyber-anything, I know, but hey . . . I mean, look,
she thinks I'm a senior at Milton, studying economics, into
John Grisham, hockey, and camping. Which is fine. Let her
think that. I do like some of those things, so what's it matter,
right? And you guys, you're still pretty positive I'm an actor,
anyway, and this is all some little show that she and I have
been rehearsing and stuff . . . but you can't be sure, can you?
I mean, not completely. When we walk out of here, a few
minutes from now, when I say, "Hey, you wanna go see the
sunset? It's beautiful out by the lake 'cause you got a clear
shot looking at it back over the mountains there . . ." you'll

Coax

just think it's a line, right? *But* is it a line that I read in my script, been practicing, or is it the same thing I say to all the women I meet, *practiced*, yes, rehearsed, absolutely, but in my room, saying it over and over while I'm jacking off, talking to some seventeen-year-old in Nebraska? Or is it both, maybe? Words from the play I'm in, from this script I'm holding here (*indicates*), but something that's started to spill over into my own conversations. You're on your own with that one; that's too much *Twilight Zone* shit for me! (*Looks offstage.*) She's coming back . . . don't say anything, okay?

He smiles as the YOUNG WOMAN *appears again.*

YOUNG WOMAN Sorry 'bout that. I just . . .

YOUNG MAN No problem, did you . . . ?

YOUNG WOMAN It's just, it's a new coat and I didn't want to get . . .

YOUNG MAN Cute.

YOUNG WOMAN Thanks. Yeah, it's . . . Agnès B.

YOUNG MAN She's a designer, right?

YOUNG WOMAN Uh-huh. You do like it?

YOUNG MAN Absolutely . . .

YOUNG WOMAN Cool.

YOUNG MAN Looks great on you. Really a nice cut . . .

YOUNG WOMAN I love her stuff. I got it . . . I shouldn't tell you . . .

YOUNG MAN What? No, go ahead . . .

YOUNG WOMAN The outlet mall. Over off 59 . . .

YOUNG MAN Really? Wow . . .

YOUNG WOMAN I know, right?! It was, like, seventy bucks is all . . . couldn't believe it. It was an imperfection, but . . .

YOUNG MAN Well, it's really nice. (*Beat.*) And you're even cuter than you said. Seriously.

YOUNG WOMAN Thanks, I . . . sorry I never sent a picture or anything, but . . .

YOUNG MAN It's okay, not a big . . .

YOUNG WOMAN But you gotta do the whole scanner thing, and then if you say you have one, people are always bugging you to give it to them and I just . . .

YOUNG MAN I understand. It's okay . . .

YOUNG WOMAN Thanks.

YOUNG MAN So . . . do you get on there much, I mean, online? Talking to people and whatever.

YOUNG WOMAN No! Hardly ever . . .

YOUNG MAN Come on . . .

YOUNG WOMAN Seriously! I don't . . . I mean, sometimes, but . . .

YOUNG MAN Nah, me either.

YOUNG WOMAN Really?

YOUNG MAN No, in fact, I just got my computer, I mean, hooked up to the Internet, like, six months ago, so . . .

YOUNG WOMAN Oh. Huh.

YOUNG MAN And I just happened to be on that night . . .

YOUNG WOMAN Yeah?

YOUNG MAN It's true . . . sometimes I'll get on there, to talk about music . . .

YOUNG WOMAN Me too.

YOUNG MAN Right, right, and then . . . we just sorta found each other.

YOUNG WOMAN Yep. (*Beat.*) It's great to finally meet you.

YOUNG MAN You too.

YOUNG WOMAN You're a little different than you described, too . . .

YOUNG MAN Really? I tried to be, you know, without being too . . .

YOUNG WOMAN A lot, actually. But I like it . . . I mean, it's even better than you said. It's nice.

Coax

YOUNG MAN Wow. Thanks . . .

YOUNG WOMAN You're very . . . anyway. It's a surprise but sweet. Most guys, even on the phone, are like, "Yes, I'm tall, tanned, sporty, and I have a huge . . ." Well, you know.

YOUNG MAN Right! I know . . . (*Laughs.*) Guys are funny . . .

YOUNG WOMAN Not that funny . . . most of the time they're just loud and weird. But you seem okay . . . more than okay.

YOUNG MAN Thanks . . .

YOUNG WOMAN I like you. I mean, so far . . .

YOUNG MAN I like you, too. I did right from the beginning, when we were first . . .

YOUNG WOMAN I know, I know, but that's so strange, the whole . . .

YOUNG MAN You're right, it is. Setting up times to meet, typing away to each other, wondering . . . this is better. (*Beat.*) So, did you tell your boyfriend or not?

YOUNG WOMAN Ummm . . . no, I didn't. I was gonna, but . . .

YOUNG MAN I totally understand. I do.

YOUNG WOMAN I mean, he'd just get all . . . you know, and that's why I always get rid of your e-mails and everything.

YOUNG MAN Not a big deal, really . . . they're private, anyway, right?

YOUNG WOMAN Yeah. I mean, it's not even like he's my boyfriend or anything, not *exclusively*, he's just funny about this kind of stuff . . .

YOUNG MAN Hey, we're just talking, right? It's only coffee.

YOUNG WOMAN Exactly. Coffee and a movie.

YOUNG MAN True. (*Beat.*) But I gotta tell you, *I* was jealous, I was, when I heard you were seeing someone.

YOUNG WOMAN I know, I should've said it right up front, but . . .

YOUNG MAN No, it's not that, it's not, I just . . . well, I thought we clicked, really early I felt that, and then when I heard about . . .

YOUNG WOMAN Jacob.

YOUNG MAN Right, right . . . Jacob . . . well, I just was like, "Damn, this guy's got it going on, this Jacob dude, because this girl is something else. She's special . . ." (*Beat.*) Anyhow, I'll put the violin away now! Sorry, God, listen to me, I'm just really happy you decided to meet up . . . that's all.

YOUNG WOMAN I agree. I like this. I'm glad you talked me into it.

YOUNG MAN Me too. (*Beat.*) Hey, you don't want anything else, do you, a muffin or something like that? Sandwich?

YOUNG WOMAN No, I'm fine . . .

YOUNG MAN Great. I'm just gonna get a check started and . . . (*Touches her hand.*) Be right back.

The YOUNG MAN *starts offstage but stops, looking at us.*

YOUNG MAN That was nice, huh? I think it went very well . . . I really do. She's totally good-looking, maybe a bit older than she said she was, but that's okay . . . and now we're gonna take off. I'm gonna go back over—after I "pay" for our drinks—and do the line about the sunset and then we're gonna take her car and drive up the road to this place I know. And that'll be that. Basically. I mean, some things'll happen, things you probably don't wanna hear—you know, *stuff*—and that's gonna be the end of our story. I mean, ol' Jacob might put up a few "missing person" posters downtown or whatever—*might* even find that he's a suspect there for a while! (*Laughs.*) But that's pretty much the whole deal. Or . . . she and I are gonna go backstage, maybe grab a drink with

friends after, and hope the reviews are good . . . You think
what you want. Whatever gets you to sleep at night. (*Looks
back at the* YOUNG WOMAN.) I'll give her a chance. I will. In
that class I took, the one I mentioned—the drama one—the
teacher told us about what the theater used to be like, not
just in places like Paris or wherever, but even here in the
States . . . I mean, people used to fight over plays, like, go
out in the street and riot and burn places down, start hitting
each other right in the aisles because they believed in this
movement or Romanticism or whatnot. Can you believe that?
I thought that was kinda neat, that it used to mean that much
to 'em . . . Nothing means shit these days. So I'm gonna give
you a chance. All your lives you've been told to shut up and
watch, just sit there, don't say anything; if you hate it, grab
your coat and leave . . . but don't *ever* say what you feel.
Don't make a scene. Well, that's fine, but it's not exactly very
passionate, either. So here's the deal . . . I'm gonna go back
over there, ask her up to the lake, and she's gonna go with
me. I promise you, she is. Whether it's in this script here, or
I'm just such a charmer, you'll have to work that out, but I'm
telling you, it's gonna happen. However . . . you guys yell loud
enough, if you call out and let her know what's going on, what
I'm about to do to her, then maybe I'll let her go. *Maybe.* I
know it sounds a bit goofy, like *Peter Pan* or some children's
show, but if you care about her enough, if you can just, just
suspend whatever the hell it is you're supposed to suspend
for a couple seconds and think about her, ask yourselves is it
worth it to look a little foolish but maybe save that girl, then
you say something. Just say it. Out loud right now and maybe
she'll hear you. What can it hurt, right? Otherwise, you're

Neil LaBute

always gonna wonder . . . (*Beat.*) Now, maybe you'll see one of
us on the subway, or at a restaurant or something and then
it'll be okay, all some great big lark . . . but if you don't, I bet
it's gonna eat at you a bit. Just a little bit.

He signals offstage for a bill and then starts back toward her.

YOUNG MAN This is it, your last chance . . . we're not gonna come
out for a curtain call, or be outside in the lobby later. This,
right now, is it. So do whatever . . .

*

(*If the audience doesn't react—the* YOUNG MAN *should smile and
shake his head, heading back toward the* YOUNG WOMAN.)

(YOUNG MAN) (Ha! You guys're worse than I am! *Cold*, man . . .)

(*If the audience does react—the* YOUNG WOMAN *should be unfazed
and wait for the* YOUNG MAN.)

(YOUNG MAN) (I was just fucking with you . . . I'm still gonna kill
'er. But it felt nice, didn't it? Saying something like that? I bet
it did . . . Yeah. And who knows, maybe next time it'll do some
good for somebody . . .)

*

He taps the YOUNG WOMAN *on the shoulder.*

YOUNG MAN Hey . . . they're getting the thing ready.
YOUNG WOMAN Great. What time's the movie?
YOUNG MAN Seven-thirty or something. Around there.
YOUNG WOMAN Great. So . . .

YOUNG MAN Right, so. So, so, so. (*Beat.*) Hey, you wanna go see the sunset? It's beautiful out by the lake 'cause you got a clear shot looking at it back over the mountains there . . .

YOUNG WOMAN Umm . . .

YOUNG MAN I mean, only if you want to. It's just . . . lovely, that's all.

YOUNG WOMAN "Lovely"? You're a smooth one . . .

YOUNG MAN Not very! So, you wanna?

She stops for a moment, studying him. Starts to speak but catches herself.

YOUNG WOMAN . . . sure. Why not?

YOUNG MAN All right, good . . . can we take your car?

YOUNG WOMAN . . . yeah, I guess. Lemme go clear off the front seat, though, it's got all my books and stuff . . ./I'm the Cabriolet around on the side.

YOUNG MAN Great. I'll just clean up our . . ./All right?

YOUNG WOMAN 'Kay. Hey, thanks for turning out so . . . I dunno. Normal.

YOUNG MAN My pleasure.

YOUNG WOMAN Cool . . . oh, one other thing, and don't hate me, okay, it's just . . . I dunno. Anyway! Look . . . my name's Anne.

YOUNG MAN Huh?

YOUNG WOMAN I'm Anne. Not Shelly. I was . . . you just hear so many stories that I . . . so there's the truth. I'm Anne./Sorry about that, I don't like lying, so . . .

YOUNG MAN It's okay . . ./I get it.

YOUNG WOMAN No, it's not, I'm just . . . I wanted to tell you before, but . . .

YOUNG MAN No problem. I understand . . . Anne.

*He reaches over and lightly kisses her cheek. She smiles and
starts off.*

YOUNG WOMAN See you in a minute. Sorry for the name thing just
then. It's, anyway, thanks. Again. You're very understanding.

YOUNG MAN No prob.

YOUNG WOMAN I like that about you.

YOUNG MAN Yeah? (*Grins.*) You like me?

YOUNG WOMAN No! I said I like that *about* you. Not you . . . but
yeah, I do. Yes. I like you. So far—even though you made me
drive *all* the way out to this . . . place. I still like you.

YOUNG MAN Ha! (*Laughs.*) That's pretty cool . . .

YOUNG WOMAN Yep, I kinda like you . . .

YOUNG MAN Well, I like you, too. I really like you . . .

YOUNG WOMAN Ha! Well then, I really *really* like you . . . so there.

*He waves and watches her go. After a moment, he begins to
gather trash.*

YOUNG MAN Okay, you win! (*To us.*) Well, you had your chance . . .
anyway, it's gonna be a really nice evening. I can tell. I know
you're all heading out to dinner after this, or for drinks or
something, but maybe you'll think about it later, tomorrow
even, and wonder if I was shitting you or not . . . who knows?
I love that, though, that uncertainty that you've got now, even
if it's only a little. Yeah, I completely get into that! It's like what
I saw in her eyes, just then, that moment when I asked about
the lake and she's studying me, noticing the J. Crew and the
good haircut and feeling okay that I'm not some Ted Bundy or
someone like that and then just jumping off the deep end with
a "Sure, why not?" To me, *that*, right there, is perfect,

Coax

untroubled happiness. When they look at you, these girls, and they suddenly trust you. Or you guys, in your little seats there, doing nothing to help her because this isn't "real" but you want to because she's cute and sweet and, you know, what if . . . ? At that moment when people're just on the edge, right on the very, very edge of it, that place between reality and illusion, and you coax them, that's all, just coax 'em a touch, and they cross over. And then it's too late . . . I love that. Yeah. *Love* it. I do. (*Smiles.*) See you around . . .

He starts off and exits. Lights slowly fade out behind him.

Silence. Darkness.

Neil LaBute

Falling in Like

Character

A WOMAN in her forties

Setting

An outdoor café on a quiet street

Silence. Darkness.

Lights up on a WOMAN *at a table, sitting quietly. After a moment,
she lets us in with a smile.*

WOMAN . . . I'm just waiting, by the way. I mean, if you're
wondering. Wondering what I'm doing here. I'm waiting.
Meeting someone. Yes. I'm not one of those people, those
types who buy a coffee or a sweet, you know what I'm saying,
who purchase one item and then sit and nurse it for, like,
three hours, reading the newspaper or a book or that type
of thing. I'm not like that. No, see, I'm meeting someone.
(*Beat.*) This is our, I don't know, whatchamacallit, our spot,
I guess. Our rendezvous, maybe. It's the—that may not be
quite right, though, "rendezvous." I'm not sure whether that
means a place or not. Does it? I'm not certain, actually; it's
one of those words that doesn't come up all that often, I
mean, like, in regular conversation—it doesn't. "Rendezvous."
So when you use it, throw it in a sentence . . . you really
should be careful. I believe it's French. I'm fairly certain,
anyway. French. But I don't know if I can use it in this case,
whether it's French or not. (*Beat.*) But you know what I'm
saying, correct? This is where we meet . . . this restaurant
here. It's our . . . Yes. Space. Or . . . *rendez-vous*, or whatever.
Uh-huh.

She checks her watch, glancing around. Smiles.

Falling in Like   119

WOMAN It's our anniversary, actually. It is . . . not, like, an official one, of course, it isn't that, but still, we're both aware of the fact and so we decided to meet here, raise a little toast to ourselves, that type of thing. I'm probably confusing you with facts, going on about . . . that's a bit of a fault of mine, going on at length to one end or another and not really . . . well, you know what I'm saying. I didn't mean to suggest that we're here every day, or that any time we go out we start here, at this table or anything, no, just that it's . . . we have a certain connection to the place because it's where we first met. (*Smiles.*) Little over a year ago and we're still . . . well, it's been very nice, that's all. It is a lovely . . . *thing* that we have here, and I'm happy. I'm quite happy with it, which you can probably tell. I adore it! (*Beat.*) And we don't try to label it or classify it as something it's not, we're taking it very slow . . . like *molasses*, if you must know . . . but it's good, no, it's very good, because that's how you tell, I mean, it's the way a person can see if something is right or not. For them and their life and just . . . everything. So it's right, that's all, and when things do come together, it works like the charm that you've always imagined life could be like. See? We've talked about this . . .

Quick check of the watch again. Waits.

WOMAN And he loves my son, which is great. It's really fantastic that he's just accepted him into his life instantly . . . allows him to come with us to movies and takes him off to the beach or one of the . . . over to a park or that type of deal—I'm taking a pottery class on Saturdays and he often jumps in, watches him during that time—it really is refreshing to see someone, a man, who's just so sure of himself, so comfortable with his own skin that he—is it "with" his own skin or "in," *in* his own skin, how does that go?—doesn't matter, whichever way you say it, that's how he is. Happy as a person. Aware as a person. *Completed* as a person. He's the most—well, I don't know—adjusted, I suppose . . . adjusted man I've ever known. And cute, too. Sexy—none of which hurts. Right? You know it doesn't . . . (*Beat.*) He's a dream, that's what he is. Dream-y.

She looks around the restaurant. Follows someone with her eyes, then back to us.

WOMAN He is . . . and it's not a flaw, it isn't, I am not saying that, but he can be . . . there are times when he's a bit late. Or . . . yes, late. There's not really another name for it. He's late. Tardy, at least. Isn't it called that, "tardy," when a person does arrive for something but they're late for it? I think that's it. They used to say that in school, and it's what I always took it to mean. That some student was late. Tardy. For classes. (*Beat.*) And he's always so nice about it, and flushed from running down the street, and he'll explain it all and it'll make total sense, complete and absolute, since this is a crazy town for traffic and the public transportation is awful, so I know what it can be like . . . I really, really do know. It's just that this is a, you know, special day—did I mention that?—so I'm hoping that he'll be . . . once or twice he just didn't show up. At all. No. I've sat at the movies before, waiting, and seen the whole film, and he's come in at the end, over the . . . you know, with the words up on the screen and the music, and been so sorry but work got in the way or that kind of thing, but

Falling in Like

that's very rare. It seems to happen less and less these days, so that's fine; as embarrassing as it can be, it's still fine. Because we're . . . we are in like. That's what he calls it. "In like." (*Smiles again.*) Isn't that sweet? I told you he's . . . he says things, some things at times that just about take your breath away, or break your heart . . . and that's where the phrase came from, "in like," because he wanted us to be sure that we knew what we were doing—we're not two kids running around the yard out back, chasing each other at *recess* . . . we are adults and we should do this right. How it's meant to be done. Like people have done it for thousands of years . . . through the ages. (*Beat.*) You meet someone, you connect or you don't, and if you do, if it's meant to be, then you fall . . . fall toward each other in a steady and true way. First in like. Then in . . . well, you know; I don't need to tell you how it goes. Or feels. And that's where we are right now . . . firmly and utterly in like. (*Lets out a loud sigh.*) Goodness! To even talk about it is, well, it's . . . yes. That. Amazing . . .

Studies her watch again. Starts to talk, then checks it one more time.

WOMAN He said on the phone that . . . he was quiet, whispering almost, and said he might be a touch late but that I should . . . and it is our anniversary, so I'm going to sit here and wait for him. Because I know he will. He *will*, absolutely and without question. (*Beat.*) You see? I have faith in him. As a man and a friend and as a person that I'm beginning to give myself to. Not because I feel good around him or that he has accepted Timmy—that's my son, Timothy, but he just hates it when I call him that, so it has to be "Timmy"—not for any reasons

Neil LaBute

like that. No. It's because I trust him. Feel like I can actually trust a man again and I do, I do trust him and care for him and just, I just . . . well, it's true. I do like him. I am in like with him. I like him so very, very much . . . and that's why I'm here right now, waiting for him. Because I am in like with the man. I am . . . (*Beat.*) I mean, just in case you were wondering . . . that's why I'm . . . Yes. I *am*. So . . .

She smiles at us again—turns slightly to watch the door.

WOMAN I'll tell you what I'm going to do: this. I'm going to give him another two minutes before I go—signal for my check and use that time to give him a chance. And he'll come, that's the thing of it, I *know* that he'll come! He always does—two minutes and he'll be here, you watch. (*Signals to the waiter.*) Well, we'll say three. Three just to be safe, and it'll take that long for them to organize the bill . . . three minutes and he will come skipping in through that door, you mark my words. Starting now . . . (*Glances at watch.*) No, wait until we're straight up and down. All right . . . and *now*. There. Three minutes. I'm serious. This is like clockwork, it is . . . here we go. I'll count it out, on the half minutes, just so you know that I'm not—you watch. Watch and learn . . . He's on his way . . . right now . . . he's just about here. I know it. I can feel it . . . He is . . . he's coming . . . yes.

She continues her vigil as the lights slowly fade.

Silence. Darkness.

Falling in Like